BEST WINE BUYS

JUDY RIDGWAY

foulsham

LONDON • NEW YORK • TORONTO • SYDNEY

foulsham

The Publishing House, Bennetts Close,
Cippenham, Berkshire, SL1 5AP, England.

ISBN 0-572-02252-2

Cover Photograph © Image Bank

Printed in Great Britain by
Cox & Wyman Ltd, Reading, Berkshire.

Contents

Preamble

*R*ather to my surprise I have been able to keep the £5.00 ceiling on the price of the majority of wines recommended in this book. However, prices have been going up and you will see that there are very few wines left on the high street which are priced under £3.00.

There are also other, even more important changes in the market place. French, Italian and French classic wines are pricing themselves out of the popular market and even the country and vin de pays wines are nudging up over the £4.00 mark. Indeed the best choice of interesting wines is now mainly to be found in the £4.00–£5.00 range.

So far, the cheaper slots are being filled with wines from Eastern Europe and rather more gradually by blended wines from South American countries like Argentina and Brazil. There are also some reasonably priced wines from Italy and Portugal. How long all these wines will remain at their current level is an open question – some Hungarian wines, for example, already cost £3.99 or more – so enjoy them now while prices are reasonable.

The so-called "flying wine-makers" continue to travel the world and, on the whole, to improve the quality of the wine with which they work. You will often see their names on the shelf descriptions or even on the labels. They include Kim Milne, Hugh Ryman, the Bright brothers and the Lurton brothers among others.

The trend towards the use of varietal labelling (including the name of the grape variety on the label) continues. You will see that wines made from Sauvignon Blanc, Chardonnay and Cabernet Sauvignon grapes are signalled in the text. But there are many other interesting grape varieties which are well worth trying.

One of these is Voignier. This grape variety originated in the northern Rhône where it is used to make the expensive and long-lasting Condrieu white wine. Now, growers in the south are using it to make spicy but very fruity wines which are ready to drink the year after they are made.

The emergence of South African wines has helped to popularise white Chenin Blanc and red Pinotage, while Argentina offers the spicy aromatic

Torrontes and California the full fruity Petite Syrah – no relation to the Rhône Syrah or Australian Shiraz.

Quite often lesser-known grape varieties are mixed with the ever-popular Chardonnay or Cabernet Sauvignon to produce a wine which will be cheaper than the pure varietal. This practice has helped to keep the New World wines on the supermarket shelves despite the increased exchange problems. Colombard, Crouchen and Chenin Blanc have joined Semillon as partners for Chardonnay and some of the blends are very successful indeed. Cabernet Sauvignon turns up with Cinsault and Ruby Cabernet as well as the more familiar Merlot and Cabernet Franc.

Sometimes you may want to buy these or other wines in larger quantities. Of course, you can just increase the number of bottles that you buy, but we have also indicated in the text those recommended wines which are also available in litre or one and a half litre sizes. There is also a separate guide to wine boxes on pages 177–187. About 80 boxes of wine are listed together with tasting notes and a rating from 1–10.

I must say that I was very pleasantly surprised by the current standard of wine in wine boxes. There were a few very sharp or acidic wines, but there were plenty of fruity wines on offer. The best were as good as anything you will find in a bottle.

Changes in price can be a problem for a book like this and so I have set out the prices in price bands £3.00–3.50, £3.50–4.00 and so on. These were as accurate as they could be at the time of going to press, so you should not get any nasty shocks when you walk into your high street store or supermarket. Indeed, you may be pleasantly surprised as many of the wines priced at £3.99 or £4.49 have been put into the category above.

Vintages can be another problem area for a book like this but because most of the wines in the book should be drunk fairly young I have decided not to bother with them. This also means that the book is not immediately out of date once the supplies from one year have run out and another vintage is substituted in the shops.

Quite often the same producers achieve consistently high scores in my tasting notes. This is because a good producer will probably make as good a wine as is possible in a bad year and a superlatively good wine in a favourable year. (If you can, it is worth trying to remember the names of the producers of the wines that you really like so that you can find them again yourself.)

Most supermarkets now have helpful shelf notes which tell you a little more about the wines on offer. You will see references to various medals and certificates of excellence and quotes from leading wine writers. All these can be helpful. But remember that at the end of the day it is what you like that counts, so don't be afraid to trust your own judgement. Be adventurous, try different wines and have fun making up your own mind which wines you want to drink.

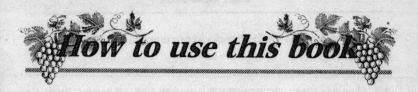

How to use this book

◆ Keep the book where you can refer to it when you are making your shopping list or store it in the glove compartment of your car and look at it in the car park.

◆ Turn to the section on the store you are visiting. You will find that the wines are arranged under headings which tell you the kind of wine to expect. Within these headings the wines are arranged in ascending order of price. Wine made from popular grape varieties such as Chardonnay and Cabernet Sauvignon are listed separately.

◆ Decide on the kind of wine you want and note down, or mark in the book, a few names of wines which fall into that category. For example, if you want a light red wine to serve at a summer barbecue look at the section headed `Light and fruity wines for easy drinking at any time' or if you are looking for a full-flavoured white wine to go with roast chicken or turkey turn to the section headed `Fuller-flavoured and fruity, but still relatively dry wines' under white wines. All the headings in the book are explained in detail on pages 8–13.

◆ If you do not have time to plan ahead, take the book into the shop with you and have a look at the wine shelves. If a particular wine catches your eye look it up in the index of the book. The index will direct you to the pages on which the wine is listed and you will be able to see which category it falls into. In most instances there will also be a short description which will help you to decide if it is the kind of wine you are looking for.

◆ If you are looking for a wine to serve at a party or a special celebration have a look at the sections headed `Good wines for parties', `Sparkling wines for aperitifs or parties' or `Splashing out'. The latter two sections include wines which cost more than the £5.00 limit set on the other sections.

◆ If you want to buy larger quantities of wine look out for the ● symbol which indicates wines which are also sold in one or one and a half litre bottles or turn to pages 177–187 on wine boxes.

◆ You will see that some wines are marked with a diamond. These are wines which I think are particularly good value in their category or which I particularly like.

◆ On those occasions when you know which wine you would like to serve you can look it up in the index to see which stores stock that wine.

White wines

Fresh and light wines for easy drinking at any time

These are dry white wines which I might choose to drink at almost any time. A very good example is Tesco Soave. These wines can be drunk on their own on a summer's day or during an evening of conversation or cards. They would make a good accompaniment to a light meal or you could serve them at a party. They are fresh but not sharp and they are usually quite uncomplicated. The Sauvignon wines probably have the most distinctive taste.

Fuller-flavoured and fruity, but still relatively dry wines

These wines are rather more complex and have a very definite character of their own. A very good example is Hardy's Nottage Hill Australian Chardonnay on sale in quite a number of outlets. The full flavour of these wines does not preclude them being drunk alone, but they will stand up to quite definite food. Some of them, like the full-blown Australian wines, make excellent aperitifs. Yet others, such as the Australian Rhine Rieslings and some Vouvrays, have a higher degree of residual sugar but do not taste as sweet as, say, German wines so I have included them in this section.

Medium dry, very fruity wines to serve at any time

The white wines in this category are medium dry in character. A very good example is Jacob Zimmermann Kabinett Pfalz from Majestic Wine Warehouses. These wines may be quite light and flowery like the German choices or they may be heavier and more distinctive. They should not be cloying. Ideally their relative sweetness is balanced by good acidity so that you are left with a pleasant non-sweet taste in the mouth. Some of them make excellent aperitifs.

Sparkling wines for aperitifs and parties

The prickle of bubbles adds a festive feel to wine. A very good example is Barramundi Australian Brut from Asda, the Co-op, Leo's and Morrisons. These wines are great for celebrations and anniversaries, but they do tend to cost rather more and so I have raised the ceiling in this category from £5.00 to £8.00.

Dessert wines

These are sweet wines to serve at the end of the meal. Like the medium dry wines they should have good balancing acidity plus a good depth of flavour. A very good example is Muscat Vin de Pays des Collines de la Maure from Thresher.

Good wines for parties

These wines are chosen both for their easy-drinking qualities and for their value. A very good example is Conca de Berbera Spanish White from Marks & Spencer. The wine you serve at a party should not be boring, but nor should it be too distinctive. If it is, some guests may not like it at all and others may not want to drink more than a couple of glasses of it. After all, not everyone likes heavily oaked white wines or very tannic reds.

Splashing out

There are some occasions when you may want to spend more than my self-imposed £5 limit. These represent just a few of the fine wines I have tasted in the high street. A very good example is Chardonnay Atesino Barrique Aged Vino da Tavola from Sainsbury.

Red wines

Light and fruity wines for easy drinking at any time

The red wines in this section correspond to the Fresh and Light category in the white wine section. A very good example is Domaine des Fontaines Merlot Vin de Pays d'Oc from Waitrose. These wines are good to drink on their own but they may also quite happily be drunk with simple, everyday meals. The alcohol levels are usually, but not always, lower than for medium or full-bodied wines.

Medium-bodied wines to serve on their own or with food

The red wines in this category are not sweet, rather they are wines which I find to be particularly versatile. A very good example is Long Mountain South African Cabernet Sauvignon from Victoria Wine shops. These wines will partner all kinds of food, but can also be served at parties or be drunk by the glass on a quiet evening at home.

Heavier wines to serve with food

As the title suggests, these wines are probably heavier in alcohol (though not always) and are likely to be more distinctive in flavour, perhaps with some oak about the place. A very good example is Safeway Casa di Giovanni Vino da Tavola di Sicilia. These wines can usually be served with well-flavoured food and indeed may be improved by the match.

Good wines for parties and Splashing out

The same criteria apply here as for white wines. Very good examples are Somerfield Côtes de Gascogne Rouge Yvon Mau for parties and Château de Beaulieu Côtes de Marmandais from Wine Cellar.

Sweetness guide

In addition to the headings outlined above, I have also included the widely used sweetness ratings which were developed by the Wine Development Board (now wound up). This guide is accepted by the EU and you may find the symbols (see page 12) used either on the supermarket shelves or on the bottle label itself.

The guide is intended to help new wine-drinkers to find their way around the most important part of the taste characteristics of white wine – the sweetness. The guide uses a scale from 1 to 9. Starting at 1, the wines are bone-dry and may be quite sharp and fresh. At 9, at the other end of the scale, are the really sweet wines.

In the middle of the scale, around 3 and 4, the acidity levels of the wine may mask the sweetness. Vinho Verde, for example, is a wine which tastes much dryer than it really is. Other wines do not seem so sweet because they are so full of rich fruit flavours. Australian Chenin Blanc and Rhine Riesling fall into this category.

BEST WINE BUYS

Bergerac
Chablis
Champagne
Dry White Bordeaux
Entre-Deux-Mers
Manzanilla Sherry
Muscadet
Pouilly Blanc Fumé
Sancerre
Saumur
Tavel Rosé
Touraine

Allela
Chardonnay from all countries
Dry English wine
Dry Montilla
Dry Sherry
Dry Sparkling wine (Brut)
Dry Vouvray
Fendant
Fino Sherry
Frascati Secco
German Trocken wines
Graves
La Mancha
Navarra
Orvieto

Pale Dry Cyprus Sherry
Penedès
Riesling d'Alsace
Rueda
Sercial Madeira
Spanish Dry White
Soave
Valencia
Verdicchio
White Burgundy
White Rhône

Brut Sparkling wine
Dry Amontillado Sherry
Dry White Vermouth
Grüner Veltliner Austrian
Halbtrocken German wines
Hungarian Olasz Rizling Dry
Medium Dry English
Medium Dry Montilla
Medium Dry Vermouth
Moseltaler
Muscat d'Alsace
Pinot Blanc d'Alsace

Golden Sherry
Demi-Sec Sparkling and Demi-Sec Champange
German Spätlesen
Tokay Szamarodni Sweet

Anjou Rosé
Australian and New Zealand Rhine Riesling
Bulgarian Olasz Rizling
Chenin Blanc
Full Amontillado
German Kabinett
German Quality wine (Qba)
Gewürtztraminer d'Alsace
Hungarian Olasz Rizling Medium Dry
Medium Dry English
Medium Dry Montilla
Medium Dry Sherry
Medium Dry Vermouth
Orvieto Abboccato
Other Gewürztraminers
Portuguese Rosé
Vinho Verde
Yugoslav Laski Rizling

Asti Spumante
Rosso, Rosé and Bianco Vermouth
Bual Madeira
German Auslesen
Monbazillac
Montilla Cream
Pale Cream Sherry
Premières Côtes de Bordeaux
Today Aszu
White Port

Barsac
Cream Cyprus Sherry
Cream Sherry
Dark Cream and Rich Cream Sherry
German and Austrian Beerenauslesen
German Eiswein
Moscatels/Muscats
Sauternes
Spanish Sweet White

Austrian Spätlese
Dry White Port
EEC Table Wine
Liebfraumilch
Medium Cyprus Sherry
Verdelho Madeira
Vouvray Demi-Sec

Brown Sherry
German and Austrian Trockenbeerenauslesen
Malaga
Malmsey Madeira
Marsala
Muscat de Beaumes de Venise

The Board also developed a red wine guide which is less widely accepted and which can be very confusing. Accordingly I have decided not to use it in my listing. However, a few outlets still use it with their shelf descriptions and so I have set out the symbols below.

It uses a simple five-point alphabetical scale. The categories attempt to identify red wine in terms of total taste or the impression that they make on the palate. Starting at A, the wines are undemanding and very easy to drink. At E, at the other end of the scale, they are bigger and have more concentrated styles. The wines here give a greater sensation of depth and fullness in the mouth.

Bardolino
Beaujolais
EEC Table wines
German Red
Touraine
Vin de Table
Vino da Tavola

Beaujolais Villages and Crus
Chinon
Côtes du Roussillon
Merlot from all countries
Navarra
Pinot Noir from all countries
Red Burgundy
Saumur
Valdepeñas
Valencia
Valpolicella
Vin de Pays

Bergerac
Bordeaux Rouge/Claret
Bulgarian Cabernet Sauvignon
Corbières
Côtes-du-Rhône
Minervois
North African Red
Rioja

Bairrada
Cabernet Sauvignon from all countries
except Bulgaria
Châteauneuf-du-Pape
Chianti
Crozes-Hermitage
Dão
Fitou
Hungarian Red
Médoc
Penedés
Ribera del Duero
Rioja Reserves
Ruby and Tawny Port

Barolo
Cyprus Red
Greek Red
Jumilla
Recioto della Valpolicella
Shiraz from Australia and South Africa

♦ = Wines which are particularly good in their price range
VdP = Vin de Pays

Best wine buys in the high street

 ## *Asda*

*T*here are 203 Asda stores scattered across the whole of the UK from Elgin in the north to St. Austell in the south.

This store has changed the arrangement of its wine shelves. Instead of being set out by country and wine region the wines are now arranged by style in grades of sweetness and fullness.

 ## *White*

Fresh and light wines for easy drinking at any time

Under £3.00	◆ Riva Trebbiano Italian White	*very fresh and fruity*	1
	Asda Sicilian Bianco		2
	Asda Hungarian Pinot Blanc	*attractive fruit*	2
	◆ Cape White South Africa	*good fruity length*	2
£3.00-3.50	● VdP des Côtes de Gascogne	*easy-drinking*	2
£3.50-4.00	Pinot Grigio Ca Pradai Grave del Friuli	*fresh and fruity*	2
£4.00-4.50	Chevalier d'Aymon Oak Aged Graves	*easy oaky fruit*	1

Lugana Sanroseda Boscaini *attractively fruity* 2

Sauvignon Blanc and Sauvignon-based wines

£3.50-4.00 ◆ Van Loveren Robertson South

African Sauvignon Blanc *particularly fruity* 1

◆ Rowan Brook Reserve Chilean

Sauvignon Blanc *gooseberry and tropical fruit* 1

£4.00-4.50 Fortant VdP d'Oc Sauvignon

Blanc *easy-drinking fruit* 2

● Bianco del Lazio Gabbia d'Oro 2

Fuller-flavoured and fruity, but still relatively dry wines

Under £3.00 Badger Hill Hungarian White *distinctive aromatic fruit* 2

● Asda Hungarian Muscat *grapey fruit* 2

Alto Plano Chilean White *distinctive citrus fruits* 1

£4.00-4.50 ◆ Fairview Estate South

African Gewürztraminer *distinctively fruity* 2

Penfolds Bin 202 Australian

Riesling 2

£4.50-5.00 Cuckoo Hill Voignier

VdP d'Oc *spicy grapefruit* 2

Hunter Cellars Bin 30

Australian White *attractively fruity* 2

Chardonnay and Chardonnay blends

£3.00-3.50 Hungarian Chardonnay Private

Reserve Mecsekalji *particularly fruity* 2

£3.50-4.00 Montagne Noire Chardonnay

VdP d'Oc *attractive boiled sweets and oak* 2

Ca Pradai Italian Chardonnay *fresh honeyed fruit* 2

Kumala Western Cape South

African Chenin/Chardonnay 2

£4.00-4.50	Cono Sur Chilean Chardonnay		2
	◆ Barramundi Australian Semillon/		
	Chardonnay	*fresh and tropical with a hint of oak*	2
£4.50-5.00	◆ James Herrick Chardonnay		
	VdP d'Oc	*full and fruity with oak*	2
	Rowan Brook Reserve Chilean		
	Chardonnay	*oaky*	2
	◆ Penfolds Bin 21 Australian		
	Semillon/ Chardonnay	*good tropical fruit*	2
	◆ Hardy's Nottage Hill		
	Australian Chardonnay	*easy-drinking tropical fruit with oak*	2
	◆ Penfolds Koonunga Hill		
	Australian Chardonnay	*particularly fruity*	2

Medium dry, very fruity wines to serve at any time

£3.00-3.50	Ruppertsberger Hofstuck		
	Riesling Kabinett	*citrus fruits*	4
	Asda Niersteiner Spiegelberg		
	Kabinett	*good fruit*	4

Sparkling wines for aperitifs and parties

£5.00-5.50	Asda Asti Spumante		7
	Asda Spanish Cava		1
£5.50-6.00	◆ Barramundi Australian Brut	*good fruit*	*2*
£6.00-6.50	◆ Cordoniu Chardonnay		
	Spanish Cava Brut	*very fruity*	2

£7.00-7.50	◆ Victoria Park Australian Pinot/Chardonnay		2

Good wines for parties

Under £3.00	● Asda Hungarian Chardonnay		2
£3.00-3.50	Jackdaw Ridge Australian Dry White	*easy-drinking*	2
£3.50-4.00	Kumala Western Cape Chenin/Chardonnay		2

Splashing out

£6.00-6.50	St Veran Domaine des Deux Roches	2

 Red and rosé

Light and fruity wines for easy drinking at any time

Under £3.00	● Asda St Chinian	*simple easy-drinking fruit*
	Riva Sangiovese di Romagna	*attractive easy fruit*
	● Valpolicella	*good fruit*
	Montepulciano d'Abruzzo Tollo	*simple, easy-drinking*
	Liubimetz Bulgarian Merlot Première	*distinctive raisiny fruit*
£3.00-3.50	◆ Santa Helena Chilean Rosé	*particularly fruity*
	Fairview South African Dry Rosé	*easy fruit*
£4.50-5.00	Hardy's Stamp Series Australian Shiraz/ Grenache Rosé	*juicy sweet fruit*

Fairview State South African
   Zinfandel/Cinsault   *good depth of fresh fruit*
◆ Stellenzict South African
   Zinfandel   *lightly oaked cherry fruit*

Medium-bodied wines to serve on their own or with food

Under £3.00	◆ Terra Alta Old Vines Garnacha	*rope, raspberries and plums*
	Romanian Pinot Noir	
£3.00-3.50	Asda Fitou	*attractive fruit*
	Asda Cape South African Red	*easy-drinking*
	Asda Californian Red	*light liquorice fruit*
£3.50-4.00	Chianti Salvanza	
£4.00-4.50	Mas Segala Côtes du Roussillon Villages	*distinctive and oaky*
	Lanskroon Estate South African Pinotage	*mature, ripe, spicy fruit*
£4.50-5.00	Domaines des Grangeneuve Coteaux du Tricastin	*attractive fruit*
	◆ Barbaresco Cantina Gemma Itàlian Red	*ripe fruit with long finish*
	Rozzano Villa Pigna Italian Red	*rich depth of oaky fruit*
	Hunter Cellars Bin 31 Australian Red	*easy-drinking ripe fruit*

Cabernet Sauvignon and Cabernet blends

Under £3.00	Asda Cabernet Sauvignon VdP d'Oc	*easy-drinking and fruity*
	● Asda Hungarian Cabernet Sauvignon	*particularly easy-drinking and fruity*
£3.00-3.50	Asda Claret	*particularly fruity*

	Bulgarian Suhindol	
	Cabernet/Merlot	*ripe distinctive fruit*
	◆ Oriachovitza Cabernet	
	Sauvignon Reserve	*rich blackcurrant and vanilla*
	◆ Rowanbrook Chilean	
	Cabernet/Malbec	*particularly fruity*
£3.50-4.00	Kumala Western Cape South	
	African Shiraz/Cabernet	*easy-drinking*
£4.00-4.50	Cono Sur Chilean Cabernet	
	Sauvignon	*intense blackcurrant jam*

Heavier wines to serve with food

£4.00-4.50	◆ Côtes du Rhône Villages	
	Domaine Beluge	*vegetal ripe fruit with chocolate*
	◆ Lehmann Vine Vale Australian	
	Shiraz	*rich leathery fruit*
	Barramundi Australian	
	Shiraz/Merlot	*warm bramble fruit*
£4.50-5.00	◆ Vacqueyras Les Cailles	*very attractive and fruity*
	◆ Rioja Crianza Campillo	*mature fruit*

Cabernet Sauvignon and Cabernet blends

£3.50-4.00	◆ Asda Chilean	
	Cabernet/Merlot	*easy-drinking blackcurrant*
£4.50-5.00	◆ Rowanbrook Reserve Chilean	
	Cabernet Sauvignon	*ripe vegetal fruit*
	◆ Penfolds Bin 35 Rawsons's	
	Retreat Australian	
	Cabernet/Shiraz	*long blackcurrant fruit*
	◆ Hardy's Nottage Hill Australian	
	Cabernet Sauvignon	*juicy red berry fruit*

BEST WINE BUYS

Good wines for parties

Under £3.00	Coltiva Il Rosso Italian Red	*easy-drinking*
	Asda Hungarian Kekfrankos	*light and simple*
£3.00-3.50	Cape Red South African	*good juicy fruit*
	Alto Plano Chilean Red	*easy-drinking fruit*

Splashing out

£7.00-7.50	◆ Quivira Californian Cabernet Cuvée	*elegant and well balanced*

Augustus Barnett

*T*his chain of off-licences was taken over by The Victoria Wine Company last year and almost all the shops have become either Victoria Wine Cellars or Victoria Wine Shops. See page 154 for the Victoria Wine Company wine list.

Berkeley Wines

*T*here are around 70 Berkeley wine shops situated in North Wales and northern England. They belong to the Greenall Cellars Group and stock about 450 wines from the Wine Cellar range (see page 170). If you cannot find one of the wines listed here in your branch of Berkeley Wines ask the manager if there is a Wine Cellar store nearby.

Bottoms Up

*T*his chain of high street off-licences is now part of the Thresher Group and many of the same wines are stocked in both stores. Because of the size of the overlap I have listed all my recommendations for both stores under Thresher on page 141.

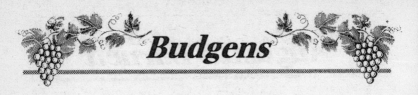

Budgens

*T*he Budgen chain now comprises 97 stores in busy high streets throughout central and southern England. There are stores as far north as Leicester and as far west as Cheddar.

The wines are arranged on the shelves by wine regions and countries. The store is currently expanding its range of wines and has already more than doubled the choice over the last year.

 *White*

Fresh and light wines for easy drinking at any time

Under £3.00	Bordeaux Blanc Sec	*fresh apples and pears* 1
£3.00-3.50	◆ Domaine de Barroque VdP des	
	Côtes de Gascogne	*fresh lemony fruit* 2
£3.50-4.00	Budgens Muscadet	1
£4.00-4.50	Tuileries du Bosc VdP de	
	Saint-Mont	2

Sauvignon Blanc and Sauvignon-based wines

£4.00-4.50	◆ Domaine Villeroy-Castellas	
	Sauvignon Blanc	*lightly herbaceous* 1
£4.50-5.00	Viña Casablanca Chilean	
	Sauvignon Blanc	*grassy citrus fruits* 2

Fuller-flavoured and fruity, but still relatively dry wines

£3.00-3.50	Clear Mountain South African Chenin Blanc	*easy-drinking pears*	2
£4.00-4.50	◆ Waimanu New Zealand White	*attractive flowery citrus fruits*	2
£4.50-5.00	High Ridge Fumé English Wine	*distinctive elderflowers and gooseberries*	2

Chardonnay and Chardonnay blends

£3.00-3.50	Chardonnay d'Oc du Lac VdP de Ile de Beauté	*perfumed flowery fruit*	2
	Bulgarian Chardonnay/ Sauvignon Blanc Preslav	*easy-drinking*	2
£3.50-4.00	Hungarian Chardonnay		2
£4.00-4.50	◆ Glen Ellen Proprietors Californian Reserve Chardonnay	*particularly fruity*	2
	Jacob's Creek Australian Semillon/Chardonnay		2
£4.50-5.00	◆ Mâcon Ige	*attractively honeyed fruit*	2
	Viña Tarapaca Chilean Chardonnay	*spicy citrus fruits*	2
	Jacob's Creek Australian Chardonnay		2

Medium dry, very fruity wines to serve at any time

| £3.50-4.00 | High Ridge English Medium Dry White | *grapefruity, minty fruit* | 4 |

Sparkling wines for aperitifs and parties

£5.00-5.50	Flinders Creek Australian Brut	2
	Flinders Creek Australian Brut Rosé	2
£6.00-6.50	Martini Italian Brut	1
£6.50-7.00	Lindauer New Zealand Brut	1

Dessert wines

£4.00-4.50	Flonheimer Adelsberg Auslese *attractively sweet raisin fruit*	5

Good wine for parties

£3.00-3.50	● Tocai del Veneto Italian White *easy-drinking apple fruit*	2

Splashing out

£6.50-7.00	Rosemount Estate Australian Chardonnay *full and fruity*	2
£10.50-11.00	Brossault Champagne	

Red

Light and fruity wines for easy drinking at any time

Under £3.00	Vin de Pays d'Agenais Rouge *good depth of fruit*	
£3.00-3.50	◆ Domaine St Roch VdP de l'Aude *ripe easy-drinking fruit*	

| £4.00-4.50 | Sutter Home Merlot | *light blackcurrant fruit* |

Cabernet Sauvignon and Cabernet blends

| Under £3.00 | Frontier Island Hungarian | |
| | Cabernet Sauvignon | *good red berry fruit* |

Medium-bodied wines to serve on their own or with food

£3.50-4.00	Faugères Maison Jeanjean	*particularly fruity*
	Costières de Nîmes	*good earthy fruity*
	Clear Mountain South African Pinotage	
£4.00-4.50	Côtes de St Mont Tuilerie du Bosc	
	Costières de Nîmes Fontanillies	*distinctive fruit*
	Pepperwood Grove Californian Zinfandel	*good red berry fruit*
	Jacob's Creek Australian Dry Red	
£4.50-5.00	◆ Château de Malijay Côtes du Rhône	*good depth of warm bramble fruit*
	Brown Brothers Australian Tarango	*particularly fruity*

Cabernet Sauvignon and Cabernet blends

£3.00-3.50	Bulgarian Cabernet Sauvignon Lyaskovets	*easy-drinking fruit*
£3.50-4.00	Budgens Claret	*easy-drinking fruit*
£4.50-5.00	◆ Viña Tarapaca Chilean Cabernet Sauvignon	*good depth of ripe fruit*

Heavier wines to serve with food

£3.00-3.50	Diego de Almagro Spanish Red	*attractive vegetal fruit*
£4.00-4.50	◆ Vina Albali Tinto Reserva Valdepeñas	*attractively mature with long ripe fruit*
£4.50-5.00	Lagunilla Rioja Reserva Crianza	*good fruit with vanilla*
	Jacob's Creek Australian Dry Red	

Cabernet Sauvignon and Cabernet blends

£4.50-5.00	Viña Casablanca Chilean Cabernet Sauvignon	

Good wines for parties

£3.00-3.50	Vin de Pays de l'Aude	*young bramble berry fruit*
	● Merlot del Veneto Italian Table Wine	*light and simple*

Splashing out

£7.00-7.50	Le Croix Teyssier St Emilion	*soft fruit with attractive length*

Cellar 5

*T*here are 250 Cellar 5 off-licence shops situated mainly in North Wales and the North of England. This chain belongs to the Greenall Cellars Group. Each store stocks around 350-400 of the Wine Cellar range (see page 170). If you have any difficulty in finding certain wines ask the manager if there is a Berkeley Wine shop or Wine Cellars store in the vicinity.

Co-op

*T*he Co-operative Wholesale Society controls 1342 stores which are scattered across the country. A wide range of wines is bought centrally by the Co-operative Wholesale Society and this list is based on those purchases. You will find all the wines at CWS retail stores.

The wines also are offered to the other Co-op retail societies and managers at each society decide which of the wines, if any, to buy. Thus you may find that your branch of the Co-op does not stock all of these wines.

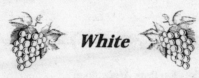

White

Fresh and light wines for easy drinking at any time

£3.00-3.50	● Co-op VdP des Côtes du Gascogne		1
	Co-op Sicilian White	*easy-drinking*	2
	Tierra Del Rey Chilean White	*gingery and herbaceous*	2
	Domaine Saint-Michel Blanc de Blanc VdP de l'Aude (vegetarian)	*apple fresh*	1
£3.50-4.00	Fair Martina Vermentino	*fresh and flinty*	1
	Co-op Pinot Grigio del Veneto	*almond fruit*	2
	Co-op Baden Dry	*particularly fruity*	2
£4.50-5.00	◆ Muscadet de Sèvre-et-Maine Domaine de la Haute		

| | Maillardière | *fresh and fruity* | 1 |

Sauvignon Blanc and Sauvignon blends

Under £3.00	Debut Bulgarian Sauvignon		
	Blanc Russe	*oaky*	1
£3.50-4.00	Co-op Bordeaux Sauvignon		
	Blanc	*light gooseberries*	1
	Touraine Sauvignon Domaine		
	du Clos de Bourg		1
	◆ Butterfly Ridge Australian		
	Sauvignon/Chenin Blanc	*fresh tropical fruit*	
		with citrus	2
£4.00-4.50	◆ Château Pierrousselle Blanc	*particularly fruity*	1
	◆ Co-op VdP d'Oc Vignerons		
	des Remparts Sauvignon		
	Blanc	*spicy herbs with*	
		gooseberries	1

Fuller-flavoured and fruity, but still relatively dry wines

Under £3.00	Mission Peak Argentinian		
	White	*easy grapey fruit*	2
	Chapel Hill Irsai Oliver	*distinctive spicy fruit*	
		with grapes	2
£3.00-3.50	◆ Hungaroo Hungarian Pinot		
	Gris	*full spicy fruit*	2
	◆ Murrumbidgee Estate Fruity		
	Australian White	*easy-drinking and, yes,*	
		it is fruity!	2
£4.00-4.50	◆ Co-op Orvieto Secco	*clover honey and*	
		greengages	2
	Penfolds Bin 202 Australian		
	Riesling	*distinctive citrus fruits*	
		and flowers	2

Chardonnay and Chardonnay blends

Under £3.00	Bear Ridge Bulgarian Chardonnay	*lightly toasty fruit*	2
£3.00-3.50	◆ Chapel Hill Hungarian Oaked Chardonnay	*lightly tropical*	2
£3.50-4.00	Co-op Chardonnay Atesino	*particularly fruity*	2
	◆ Kirkwood Moldovan Chardonnay	*easy-drinking oaky fruit*	2
	◆ Co-op Jacaranda Hill Australian Semillon/Chardonnay	*tropical fruit*	2
	◆ Kingston Estate Australian Colombard/Chardonnay	*fresh and fruity*	2
	Long Slim Chilean Chardonnay/Semillon		2
	Oak Village South African Chardonnay	*lush fruit*	2
£4.00-4.50	VdP d'Oc Chardonnay Fleur du Moulin	*simple and easy-drinking*	2
	◆ Italian Chardonnay del Salento	*particularly fruity*	2
	◆ Barramundi Australian Semillon/Chardonnay	*fresh and tropical with a hint of oak*	2
	Jacob's Creek Australian Semillon/Chardonnay		2
	◆ Lindemans Cawarra Colombard/Chardonnay	*lightly tropical with good finish*	2
£4.50-5.00	◆ Alasia Italian Chardonnay	*fresh but buttery fruit*	2
	◆ Hardy's Nottage Hill Australian Chardonnay	*easy-drinking tropical fruit with oak*	2

Penfolds Bin 21 Australian
Semillon/Chardonnay   2

Medium dry, very fruity wines to serve at any time

£3.00-3.50	Co-op Oppenheimer Krotenbrunnen		5
£3.50-4.00	◆ Devil's Rock Riesling	*fresh and grapefruity*	3

Sparkling wines for aperitifs and parties

£4.50-5.00	◆ Co-op Asti Spumante Italian Sparkling Wine	*grapey fruit*	7
£5.00-5.50	Co-op Spanish Cava	*good earthy fruit*	2
£5.50-6.00	◆ Barramundi Australian Sparkling Wine	*very good fruit*	2
£6.50-7.00	Co-op Sparkling Saumur	*particularly fruity*	2

Dessert wines

£4.00-4.50	◆ Kirchheimer Schwarzerde Beerenauslese (half)	*fresh citrus and raisins*	8
	◆ Monbazillac Domaine du Haut Rauly (half)	*particularly fruity*	8

Good wines for parties

Under £3.00	● Co-op Vino da Tavola Bianco	*soft honeyed fruit*	2
	Co-op Australian White	*simple and easy-drinking*	2

£3.50-4.00	Namacqa South African		
	Colombard	*fresh and fruity*	2

£6.00-6.50	Cathedral Cellar South African		
	Chardonnay	*good oaky fruit*	2
£7.50-8.00	◆ Chablis Les Vignerons de		
	Chablis		1

 Red

£3.00-3.50	◆ Co-op Côtes du Roussillon	*easy-drinking and fruity*
	Co-op Principato Valdadige	
	Italian Rosso	*particularly fruity*
	Tiera del Rey Chilean Red	*simple and easy-drinking*
	Hungaroo Hungarian Merlot	*vegetal fruit*
£3.50-4.00	Domaine Conquet Merlot	
	VdP d'Oc	*rich vegetal fruit*
	Balbi Vineyards Argentinian	
	Syrah Rosé	*good berry fruit*
£4.00-4.50	L.A. Cetto Mexican Petite	
	Syrah	*full easy-drinking fruit*

Cabernet Sauvignon and Sauvignon blends

£3.00-3.50	Co-op VdP d'Oc Cabernet	
	Sauvignon	
	◆ Kirkwood Moldovan	
	Cabernet/Merlot	*full easy-drinking fruit*

Medium-bodied wines to serve on their own or with food

Under £3.00 ● ◆	Co-op Vino da Tavola Rosso	fresh but vegetal fruit
	Co-op Cape South African Red	easy-drinking and fruity
£3.00-3.50	Co-op VdP d'Oc Syrah	easy chocolatey fruit
£3.50-4.00 ◆	Co-op Dão	attractively full and fruity
	Bad Tempered Cyril Tempranillo/Syrah VdP d'Oc	earthy fruit
	Co-op Montepulciano d'Abruzzo	ripe berry fruit with good length
	Oak Village South African Pinotage	fresh and fruity
£4.00-4.50	Château Berbeau St Chinian	meaty fruit
	Barramundi Australian Shiraz/Merlot	attractive mellow fruit
£4.50-5.00	Cape Afrika Pinotage	long mature fruit

Cabernet Sauvignon and Cabernet blends

Under £3.00 ●	Russe Bulgarian Cabernet/ Cinsault	tannic fruit
£3.50-4.00	Russe Reserve Bulgarian Cabernet	long ripe fruit
	Co-op Chilean Cabernet Sauvignon Curico Valley	good fruit
	Long Slim Chilean Cabernet/ Merlot	
£4.00-4.50 ◆	Château Pierrouselle Bordeaux	particularly fruity
	Amazon Cabernet Sauvignon	full flavoured mixed berry fruit

Robertson South African
Cabernet *good depth of fresh blackcurrant fruit*

Heavier wines to serve with food

£3.00-3.50	Co-op Spanish Tempranillo *oaky*
£3.50-4.00	Co-op Bairrada Portuguese Red
	Kingston Estate Shiraz/Mataro *warm leathery fruit*

Cabernet Sauvignon and Cabernet blends

£3.50-4.00	◆ Co-op Jacaranda Hill Australian Shiraz/Cabernet *particularly fruity*
£4.00-4.50	Co-op Australian Cabernet Sauvignon
	Hardy's Stamp Series Australian Shiraz/Cabernet
	Jacob's Creek Australian Shiraz/Cabernet
£4.50-5.00	Penfolds Bin 35 Australian Shiraz/Cabernet

Good wines for parties

Under £3.00	◆ Debut Bulgarian Merlot Svischtov *easy-drinking fruit with good depth*
	Marques de la Sierra Spanish Garnacha *attractive easy-drinking*
	Mission Peak Argentinian Red Mendoza *easy-drinking warm fruit*
	Tierra del Rey Chilean Red *easy-drinking*

Splashing out

£5.50-6.00   ◆ Vacqueyras Cuvée du Marquis
de Fonseguille

£6.50-7.00   ◆ Morgon Les Charmes Domaine
Brisson   *good meaty fruit*

Cullens

*T*here are 24 shops in the SouthEast and London area and the home counties which have a fairly limited range of wines.

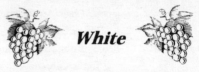

White

Fresh and light wines for easy drinking at any time

£3.50-4.00	Castillo di Liria Spanish Dry White	2
£4.00-4.50	Muscadet de Sèvre-et-Maine	1
£4.50-5.00	Pinot Grigio del Veneto	2

Fuller-flavoured and fruity, but still relatively dry wines

£4.00-4.50	Blossom Hill California Dry White	2

Chardonnay and Chardonnay blends

£4.50-5.00   Hardy's Stamp Australian
                   Semillon/Chardonnay   *particularly fruity*   2
             Jacob's Creek Australian
                   Chardonnay   2

Sparkling wine

£7.00-7.50   Sea View Australian Brut   2

Good wine for parties

£3.00-3.50   Bulgarian Country Wine
                   Muskat and Ugni Blanc   *easy-drinking*   3

Splashing out

£5.50-6.00   Star Sutter Home Californian
                   Chardonnay   *lightly tropical fruit
                        with apples*   2
£6.00-6.50   Star Nottage Hill Australian
                   Chardonnay   *easy-drinking tropical
                        fruit with oak*   2
             Star Penfolds Koonunga Hill
                   Australian Chardonnay   *particularly fruity*   2

Red

Light and fruity wine for easy drinking at any time

£4.00-4.50   Blossom Hill Californian Dry Red

Medium-bodied wines to serve on their own or with food

Cabernet Sauvignon and Cabernet blends

£4.50-5.00 ◆ Mauregard Rouge Petit
Château   *well balanced fruit and*
                                        tannin

Heavier wines to serve with food

Cabernet Sauvignon and Cabernet blends

£4.50-5.00   Jacob's Creek Australian
Shiraz/Cabernet

Good wine for parties

£3.50-4.00   Merlot del Veneto   *easy-drinking*

Splashing out

£6.00-6.50 ◆ Nottage Hill Australian
Cabernet Sauvignon   *juicy red berry fruit*

*T*here are 77 specialist wine shops in the Davison chain. They are scattered over most of London and the home counties. The wines are arranged on the shelves by area and country.

White

£3.00-3.50	Servus Burgenland Austrian White	*easy-drinking*	3
£3.50-4.00	Cape Cellars South African Colombard		2
£4.00-4.50	VdP des Côtes de Gascogne Colombard		3
	Muscadet de Sèvre-et-Maine Pierre Millot		1
	◆ Nuragus di Cagliari	*particularly fruity*	1
	Frascati Secco Superiore Ambra		2
£4.50-5.00	◆ Torres Vina Sol Spanish White	*fresh and fruity*	1

Sauvignon Blanc and Sauvignon blends

£4.00-4.50	Bordeaux Sauvignon Blanc		1
£4.50-5.00	South African Sauvignon Blanc KWV		1

Fuller-flavoured and fruity, but still relatively dry wines

£3.00-3.50	Muscat/Ugni Blanc Bulgarian Country Wine	*easy-drinking*	3
£4.00-4.50	South African Chenin Blanc KWV		2
£4.50-5.00	Nobilo White Cloud New Zealand Müller-Thurgau/ Sauvignon Blanc	*distinctively fruity*	2

Chardonnay and Chardonnay blends

£4.00-4.50	Lindeman Cawarra Australian Semillon/Chardonnay		
	Hardy's Stamp Series Australian Semillon/Chardonnay	*particularly fruity*	2
£4.50-5.00	◆ James Herrick Chardonnay VdP d'Oc	*full and fruity with oak*	2
	Domaine de Pierre Jacques Chardonnay VdP d'Oc		2
	◆ Sutter Home Chardonnay	*lightly tropical fruit with apples*	3
	Cook's New Zealand Chardonnay		3
	◆ Hardy's Nottage Hill Australian Chardonnay	*easy-drinking tropical fruit with oak*	2
	◆ Penfolds Rawson Retreat Semillon/Chardonnay	*full fruit*	2

Medium dry, very fruity wines to serve at any time

£4.00-4.50	● Piesporter Michelsberg		3
	Niersteiner Gutes Domthal Edward Wolf		3

38

£4.50-5.00   Hardy's RR Medium   *full and fruity*   4

Sparkling wines for aperitifs and parties

£5.00-5.50	Clair Diamant Blanc de Blanc Brut	1
£5.50-6.00	Killawarra Australian Brut	2
£6.00-6.50	Angas Australian Brut	2
	Seaview Australian Brut	2
£7.00-7.50	Asti Martini Italian Sparkling Wine	5
	Lindauer New Zealand Sparkling Wine	2

Dessert wines

£4.50-5.00   ◆ French Muscat José Sala   *grapey fruit*   5

Good wines for parties

£3.50-4.00   Cape Cellars South African Sauvignon Blanc   1

Splashing out

£6.00-6.50   ◆ Rothbury Estate Chardonnay   *long elegant fruit*   2

Red

Light and fruity wines for easy drinking at any time

£3.00-3.50	Castillo de Liria Spanish Red	*easy-drinking*
	Bulgarian Merlot	
£4.00-4.50	Valpollicella Zonin	*pleasantly fruity*
£4.50-5.00	Domaine de Limbardie VdP	
	des Coteaux de Murviel	
	Peter Lehmann Australian	
	Grenache	*easy-drinking summer berries*

Medium-bodied wines to serve on their own or with food

£3.50-4.00	Don Gulias Spanish Vino de Mesa	
£4.00-4.50	Domaine de la Masette VdP	
	de l'Hérault	
	Côtes du Roussillon Villages	
	South African Pinotage KWV	
£4.50-5.00	Sutter Home California	
	Merlot	*light blackcurrant fruit*

Cabernet Sauvignon and Cabernet blends

£3.00-3.50	Bulgarian Country Wine	
	Cabernet/Merlot	*fruity and easy-drinking*
	Svischtov Bulgarian Cabernet	
	Sauvignon	
£4.00-4.50	Bordeaux Rouge House Claret	
	Bulgarian Reserve Cabernet	
	Sauvignon Russe	
£4.50-5.00	Caliterra Chilean Cabernet	
	Sauvignon	*good depth of blackcurrant fruit*

Sutter Home Californian
Cabernet Sauvignon   *good fruit*

Heavier wines to serve with food

£3.50-4.00   Terras d'El Rei Portuguese Tinto
Cabernet Sauvignon and Cabernet blends
£4.00-4.50 ◆ Hardy's Stamp Series Australian
Shiraz/Cabernet   *easy-drinking*
£4.50-5.00   Jacob's Creek Australian
Shiraz/Cabernet
Hardy's Nottage Hill Australian
Cabernet Sauvignon   *juicy berry fruit*
Penfolds Bin 35 Rawsons
Retreat Shiraz/Cabernet   *long easy-drinking fruit*

Good wines for parties

£3.50-4.00 ◆ Via Nova Merlot del Veneto   *attractively fruity*
Hungarian Cabernet Sauvignon
Minosegi Bor

Splashing out

£5.50-6.00   Marquès de Caceres Rioja Tinto
◆ Penfolds Koonunga Hill Shiraz/
Cabernet   *good depth of long fruit*

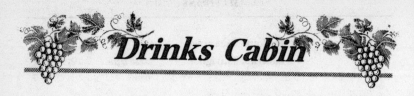

Drinks Cabin

'*D*rinks Stores from Thresher' shops are to be relaunched as 'Drinks Cabin' shops. The 400 local stores have started changing their names and the changeover should be complete shortly.

The wines stocked in Drinks Cabin stores come from the Thresher cellars so check the Thresher entry on page 141. Of course, Drinks Cabins Stores are smaller then Thresher Wine Shops and so will not stock the full range. If you cannot find the wine you want ask the manager to direct you to the nearest Thresher store.

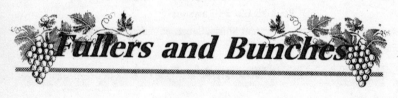

Fullers and Bunches

*T*here are 70 Fullers wine shops concentrated in London and the home counties. The wines are organised by country and wine region.

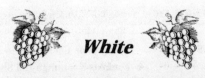

White

Fresh and light wines for easy drinking at any time

£3.00-3.50   Castillo de Mont Blanc Conca de Barbera Spanish White *fresh and easy-drinking*   2

£3.50-4.00	● Le Gascony Côtes des Gascogne	*particularly fruity*	2
£4.00-4.50	◆ Muscat del Salento Le Trulle	*fresh and grapey*	2
£4.50-5.00	◆ Châteaux Haut Grelot Bordeaux Blanc	*minty and herbaceous*	1
	◆ Can Feixes Penedès	*attractively fresh and fruity*	2

Sauvignon Blanc and Sauvignon blends

£3.50-4.00	Terret/Sauvignon VdP d'Oc Lurton	*spicy herbs*	1
	◆ Côtes de Duras Sauvignon Blanc Berticot	*elegant gooseberry fruit*	1
£4.00-4.50	Sauvignon VdP d'Oc Lurton	*minty gooseberries*	1
	Touraine Sauvignon le Barbottes	*honeyed and herbaceous*	1
£4.50-5.00	◆ Bellingham South African Sauvignon	*green herby gooseberries*	1

Fuller-flavoured and fruity, but still relatively dry wines

£3.00-3.50	Eagle Mountain Irsai Oliver	*distinctive fruit*	1
	Eagle Mountain Harslevelu	*grapefruit/orange zest fruit*	2
£3.50-4.00	Argentinian Torrontes Jacques Lurton Mendoza	*spicy grapes*	2
£4.50-5.00	Domaine de Raissac Voignier VdP de l'Aude	*peachy fruit*	2

Chardonnay and Chardonnay blends

£3.50-4.00	Chardonnay VdP du Jardin de la France	*easy-drinking*	2

	Khan Krum Bulgarian		
	Chardonnay Reserve	*oaky*	2
	Gyongyos Hungarian		
	Chardonnay	*lightly tropical*	2
£4.00-4.50	Tocornal Chardonnay	*easy-drinking and*	
		lightly tropical	2
	◆ Lindemans Cawarra Australian		
	Semillon/Chardonnay	*lightly tropical with*	
		a good finish	2
£4.50-5.00	◆ James Herrick Chardonnay		
	VdP d'Oc	*full and fruity with*	
		oak	2
	◆ Santa Ines Barrel Fermented		
	Chilean Chardonnay	*well balanced fruit*	
		with good oak	2
	◆ Caliterra Chilean Chardonnay	*smoky tropical fruit*	2
	◆ Valdivieso Chilean Reserve		
	Chardonnay	*rich and oaky*	2
	◆ Penfolds Bin 21 Australian		
	Semillon/Chardonnay	*good tropical fruit*	2
	◆ Hardy's Nottage Hill Australian		
	Chardonnay	*easy-drinking tropical*	
		fruit with oak	2

Medium dry, very fruity wines to serve at any time

Under £3.00	Muskat & Ugni Blanc Bulgarian		
	Country Wine	*easy-drinking*	3
£3.00-3.50	Wiltinger Scharzberg Riesling		
	Kabinett		4
£4.50-5.00	◆ Hardy's "RR" Australian		
	White	*distinctively fruity*	3

Sparkling wines for aperitifs and parties

£5.50-6.00	Yalumba Killawarra Australian Rosé	3
£6.00-6.50	Angas Brut Australian Rosé	2
£6.50-7.00	Blanquette de Limoux	2

Dessert wines

£3.50-4.00	Castillo di Liria Moscatel de Valencia	*distinctively fruity*	5
£4.00-4.50	◆ Kirchheimer Schwarzerde Beerenauslese Zimmermann Graeff (half)	*dried apricots and citrus fruits*	7

Good wines for parties

£3.00-3.50	Winter Hill VdP de l'Aude	*apple fresh*	1
	Preslav Bulgarian Chardonnay		2

Splashing out

£5.00-5.50	◆ Rothbury Estate South Eastern Australian Chardonnay	*lush and long*	2
£6.00-6.50	◆ Chardonnay de Salento Vigneto di Caramia	*full and fruity with well balanced oak*	2

Red and rosé

Light and fruity wines for easy drinking at any time

£3.00-3.50	Suhindol Bulgarian Merlot	*particularly fruity*
£3.50-4.00	◆ Carignan Vieilles Vignes	
	VdP d'Oc Lurton	*deep plum and bramble fruit*
	Domaine de Serame Merlot	
	Lurton	*easy-drinking, lightly vegetal fruit*
	Merlot Atesino Concilio	*easy-drinking*
	Puglian Rosé Cantele	*attractive fruit*
£4.00-4.50	Teroldego Rotaliano	
	Italian Red	*particularly fruity*
	◆ Thornhill Californian Barbera	*easy-drinking red currant fruit*

Medium-bodied wines to serve on their own or with food

£3.00-3.50	J.P.Tinto Portuguese Red	*distinctive chewy coffee fruit*
	Casa de la Vina Spanish	
	Cencibel Valdepeñas	*sweet ripe fruit*
£3.50-4.00	◆ Montagne Noire Syrah VdP	
	d'Oc	*well balanced fruit*
£4.00-4.50	◆ Castilla de Manzares Cabernet	
	Sauvignon La Mancha	*attractive full ripe fruit*
	◆ Montepulciano d'Abruzzo	
	Barrique Casal Bordino	*attractive fruit with good length*
	◆ Argentinian Malbec/	
	Tempranillo	*attractive mixed berry fruit*

	◆ Concha y Toro Chilean	
	Merlot	*ripe fruit with black-currants and brambles*
£4.50-5.00	Cono Sur Chilean Pinot Noir	*Warm vegetal fruit*

Cabernet Sauvignon or Cabernet blends

£3.00-3.50	● Bulgarian Cabernet Sauvignon Suhindol	
£3.50-4.00	Cabernet/Syrah Limouxins VdP d'Oc	
	Oriachovitza Bulgarian Cabernet Sauvignon Reserve	
£4.00-4.50	◆ Tierra Secca Tempranillo/Cabernet La Mancha	*easy-drinking red berry fruit*
	Isla Negra Chilean Cabernet Cono Sur	*long and fruity*
	Santa Ines Chilean Cabernet/Merlot	*attractive milky fruit*

Heavier wines to serve with food

£4.00-4.50	Toconal Chilean Merlot	*particularly fruity*
£4.50-5.00	Torres Coronas Penedès Spanish Red	
	Bellingham South African Shiraz	*attractively fruity*
	Penfolds Bin 2 Shiraz/Mourvedre	*warm blackberries and blackcurrants*

Good wines for parties

| £3.00-3.50 | ◆ Winter Hill VdP de l'Aude | *fresh and fruity* |

	Castillo de Mont Blanc Conca de Barbera	*fresh cherry fruit*
	Eagle Mountain Kekfrankos	*light and easy-drinking fruit*
£3.50-4.00	Belfont VdP de l'Aude	*easy-drinking*

Splashing out

£5.50-6.00	◆ Châteaux Gazeau Bordeaux Supérieur	*mellow fruit with cedarwood*
£6.00-6.50	◆ Woolshed Coonawarra Australian Red (Cabernet/Shiraz/Merlot)	*fresh juicy fruit with good length*
	Côtes du Rhône Jean Luc Colombo	*Good fruit*

Gateway

*T*hese stores are owned by Somerfield Stores Limited and as they are modernised they will be changing their names to Somerfield. There are currently 250 stores still carrying the Gateway name. For details of their wines see the entry for Somerfield on page 119.

Greenall Food Stores

*T*hese shops are part of the Greenall Cellars Group. Each store stocks around 200 of the wines from the Wine Cellar list (see page 170). If you cannot find the wine you want in your local branch ask the manager if there is a Berkeley Wine store or Wine Cellar store nearby.

KwikSave

*T*he alcoholic arm of KwikSave is known as LiquorSave. There are almost 1000 licenced stores spread across the UK.

The wine buyers at this store have been working hard to find interesting wines at very reasonable prices. Last year they said that they hoped to have an even better range of wines this year and they have succeeded. There is a good range of attractive wines under £3.00.

 White

Fresh and light wines for easydrinking at any time

Under £3.00	Juan Carillo Spanish White	*attractively fresh*	2
	California Cellars White		2
£3.00-3.50	Frascati	*very fresh*	1
	Sauvignon Blanc or Sauvignon blends		
Under £3.00	Bordeaux Sauvignon Cuvée V.E.	*lightly herby*	1
	White Pacific Chilean Sauvignon	*fulsome gooseberries*	*1*

Fuller-flavoured and fruity, but still relatively dry wines

Under £3.00 ◆	Khan Krum Riesling & Dimiat	*fruity and fresh*	2

| | Hungarian Country Wine | *fresh and easy-drinking* | 2 |
| | Hungarian Pinot Gris | *fresh and fruity* | 2 |

Chardonnay or Chardonnay blends

Under £3.00	Hungarian Chardonnay	*lightly tropical*	2
	◆ Preslav Bulgarian Chardonnay/Sauvignon	*fresh and fruity*	2
£3.00-3.50	Skylark Hill Chardonnay VdP d'Oc	*honeyed fruit*	1
	◆ Gandia Hoya Valley Spanish Chardonnay	*good depth of well balanced fruit*	2
£3.50-4.00	◆ Angoves's Classic Reserve Australian Chardonnay	*oaky, lemony fruity*	2

Medium dry, very fruity wines to serve at any time

Under £3.00	Mosel Linden		3
	Clearsprings South African Cape White		4
	Valley Home Riesling St Ursula	*fresh and fruity*	2

Sparkling wines for aperitifs and parties

| **£4.50-5.00** | ◆ Spanish Cava Brut | *good fruit* | 2 |
| **£5.50-6.00** | Asti Martini | | 7 |

Dessert wines

| **£3.00-3.50** | ◆ Castillo de Liria Moscatel | *distinctively fruity* | 8 |

Good wines for parties

Under £3.00 VdP de l'Hérault   *fresh and fruity*
Pelican Bay Australian
   Medium Dry White   *easy-drinking fruit*   2

Splashing out

£9.00-9.50 Louis Raymond Champagne   1

 Red

Light and fruity wines for easy drinking at any time

Under £3.00 Rosé de France   *easy-drinking boiled*
                                          sweets

VdP de l'Hérault
Grenach Gris VdP d'Oc Rosé *pretty fruit*
Skylark Hill Merlot   *easy-drinking soft fruit*
Valpolicella   *cherry fruit*
Clearsprings South African
Cape Red
£3.50-4.00 ◆ Côtes de Malepère Domaines
   des Bruyères   *attractive fruit with a*
                         touch of raspberries

Medium-bodied wines to serve on their own or with food

Under £3.00 ◆ Montepulciano d'Abbruzzo   *good depth of attractive*
                                            fruit

Flamenco Carinena Spanish
   Red   *reasonable fruit*

	Bulgarian Reserve Merlot	
	Domaine Sakar	*hot ripe fruit*
	Romanian Young Vatted	
	Merlot	*good fruit*
£3.00-3.50	◆ Côtes du Rhône	*easy-drinking and fruity*
	Pelican Bay Australian Red	
£3.50-4.00	Tempranillo Berberana Rioja	*good fruit*

Cabernet Sauvignon and Cabernet blends

Under £3.00	Cabernet Sauvignon VdP d'Oc	*very dry*
	Bulgarian Merlot/Cabernet	
	Sauvignon Liubimetz	*good ripe fruit*
	Bulgarian Lovico Suhindol	
	Bulgarian Cabernet/Merlot	
£3.00-3.50	Skylark Hill Cabernet Sauvignon/	
	Shiraz VdP d'Oc	*good depth*
	Bordeaux Claret Cuvée VE	
	◆ Bulgarian Sauvignon Reserve	
	Elhovo	*mature warm fruit*
£3.50-4.00	Butterfly Ridge Australian	
	Cabernet/Shiraz	*fresh, juicy fruit*

Heavier wines to serve with food

Under £3.00	Alta Mesa Portuguese Red	*hot and raisiny*
	José Neiva Portuguese Red	*mature cakey fruit*
£3.50-4.00	Angoves Australian Reserve	
	Shiraz	*bramble and blackcurrant fruit*

Good wines for parties

Under £3.00	Les Garrigues VdP des	
	Cevennes	*simple and easy-drinking*

	Mendoza Argentinian Red	
	Lurton	*easy sweet fruit*
£3.00-3.50	Bulgarian Reserve Gamza	*easy-drinking*

Leo's

*T*his is the chain operated by Co-operative Retail Services, the second largest of the retail co-operative societies. Its geographical coverage takes in the West Country, Wales and the North West as well as London and the South East. Pioneer and Lo-Cost stores are part of the same group and there are 214 stores in total.

This wine list contains some Co-op wines but most are bought by Leo's own wine buying team. The full range can be found in the larger stores with a slightly reduced range available in smaller stores.

White

Fresh and light wines for easy drinking at any time			
£3.00-3.50	Co-op VdP des Côtes de Gascogne		2
£3.50-4.00	◆ Château du Plantier Entre-deux-Mers	*good depth of attractive fruit*	2
	Namacqa Colombard Vrendenal	*easy honeyed fruit*	2
£4.00-4.50	Marquès de Caceres White Rioja		2
	Torres Vina Sol Spanish White	*well balanced fruit*	1

Sauvignon Blanc and Sauvignon blends

£3.50-4.00	◆ Bordeaux Sauvignon St-Vincent	*attractive herby fruit*	1
£4.00-4.50	◆ Miguel Torres Santa Digna Chilean Sauvignon Blanc	*wonderfully fresh and ripe grassy herbaceous fruit*	1

Fuller-flavoured and fruity, but still relatively dry wines

£3.00-3.50	Hungarian Muscat Ottonel Nagyrede	*soft grapey fruit*	2
	Chapel Hill Irsai Oliver	*distinctive spicy fruit with grapes*	2
£3.50-4.00	◆ Hungaroo Hungarian Pinot Gris	*full spicy fruit*	2
£4.00-4.50	◆ Co-op Orvieto Secco	*clover honey and greengages*	2
	Cafayete Argentinian Torrontes Etchart	*distinctively aromatic and minty fruit*	2
	Cuckoo Hill Southern French Voignier VdP d'Oc	*spicy grapefruit*	2
	◆ Penfolds Bin 202 Australian Riesling	*distinctive citrus fruits and flowers*	3

Chardonnay and Chardonnay blends

Under £3.00	◆ Gandia Hoya Valley Spanish Chardonnay Utiel Requena	*good depth of well balanced fruit*	2
£3.00-3.50	Atesino Italian Chardonnay	*particularly fruity*	2

£4.00-4.50	Cuckoo Hill Southern French		
	Chardonnay VdP d'Oc	*easy-drinking apples and pears*	2
◆	Van Loveren Spes Bona South		
	African Chardonnay	*attractively fresh and fruity*	2
◆	Barramundi Australian Semillon/		
	Chardonnay	*fresh and tropical with a hint of oak*	2
	Hardy's Stamp Series Australian		
	Semillon/Chardonnay	*tropical fruit*	2
£4.50-5.00 ◆	Cuckoo Hill Southern French		
	Barrel Fermented		
	Chardonnay VdP d'Oc	*good depth of fruit*	2
◆	Sutter Home Californian		
	Chardonnay	*lightly tropical fruit with apples*	3
◆	Hardy's Nottage Hill		
	Australian Chardonnay	*easy-drinking tropical fruit with oak*	2
	Rosemount Estate Semillon/		
	Chardonnay	*restrained tropical fruits*	2

Medium dry, very fruity wines to serve at any time

£3.00-3.50	Carl Reh Binger		
	St Rochuskapelle	*spicy flowery fruit*	4

Sparkling wines for aperitifs and parties

£5.50-6.00 ◆	Barramundi Australian		
	Sparkling Wine	*very good fruit*	2

£6.00-6.50	Asti Martini		5
	Seaview Australian Brut OZ		2
£6.50-7.00	Condorniu Spanish Cava		2
£7.50-8.00	◆ Bouvet Saumur Brut	*biscuity fruit*	2

Dessert wines

£3.50-4.00	Dom Brial Muscat de Rivesaltes (half)	*almonds and grapey fruit*	7

Good wines for parties

Under £3.00	Castillo de Liria Valencia Spanish White		2
£3.00-3.50	Chenin Blanc Les Fleurs VdP du Jardin de la France	*soft and easy*	2
	Co-op Australian White	*easy-drinking simple fruit*	2

Splashing out

£6.00-6.50	◆ Château Tahbilk Marsanne	*tropical fruits and citrus*	2

Red

Light and fruity wines for easy drinking at any time

£3.00-3.50	◆ Co-op Côtes du Roussillon	*easy-drinking and fruity*
	Co-op Principato	*particularly fruity*
	◆ Gandia Hoya Valley Merlot Utiel	*very attractive soft fruit*

	Vina Albali Tempranillo	
	Valdepeñas	*fresh berry fruit*
	Prahova Valley Romanian	
	Pinot Noir	*full, ripe flavours*
£4.00-4.50	Cuckoo Hill Southern French	
	Merlot VdP d'Oc	*full easy-drinking fruit*
£4.50-5.00	L.A. Cetto Mexican Petite	
	Sirah	*full easy-drinking fruit*

Medium-bodied wines to serve on their own or with food

£3.00-3.50	◆ Fitou Madame Claude	
	Parmentier	*good depth of fruit*
	Domaine de Borios Saint	
	Chinian	*easy-drinking fruit*
	Château du Bosc Coteaux du	
	Languedoc	*particularly fruity*
	◆ Co-op Dão	*attractively full and fruity*
£3.50-4.00	Domaine de Barjac VdP du	
	Gard (organic)	*particularly fruity*
	Celliers des Dauphins Côtes	
	du Rhône	
	Co-op Montepulciano	
	d'Abruzzo	*ripe berry fruity with*
		good length
£4.00-4.50	Cuckoo Hill Southern French	
	Cabernet/Merlot VdP d'Oc	*hot blackcurrant fruit*

Cabernet Sauvignon and Cabernet blends

£3.00-3.50	◆ Romanian Special Reserve	
	Cabernet Sauvignon	*easy-drinking fresh fruit*
£3.50-4.00	Co-op Curico Valley Chilean	
	Cabernet Sauvignon	*good fruit*
£4.00-4.50	◆ Château Pierrousselle	*particularly fruity*

Heavier wines to serve with food

£3.00-3.50	Co-op Bairrada Portuguese Red
£3.50-4.00	Co-op Rioja Tinto
£4.00-4.50	◆ Lehmann Vale Vine Shiraz *rich leathery fruit*

Cabernet Sauvignon and Cabernet blends

£3.00-3.50	◆ Oriachovitza Cabernet Sauvignon Reserve	*rich blackcurrant and vanilla*
£4.00-4.50	◆ Hardy's Stamp Series Australian Shiraz/Cabernet	*easy-drinking*
	Jacob's Creek Australian Shiraz/Cabernet	
£4.50-5.00	◆ Hardy's Nottage Hill Australian Cabernet Sauvignon	*juicy red berry fruit*
	Rosemount Estate Australian Shiraz/Cabernet	*good depth of leathery fruit*

Good wines for parties

Under £3.00	● Castillo de Liria	*easy-drinking*
	Blossom Hill Californian Red	
£3.00-3.50	Bottichio Vino da Tavola di Sicilia Rosso Firriato	*simple easy-drinking wine*
	Chapel Hill Cabernet Sauvignon	*light and simple wine with raspberries*

Lo-Cost

*T*his chain of stores is part of Co-operative Retail Services and the wines stocked are similar to those listed for Leo's (see page 55).

 # *Londis*

*T*here are around 1500 Londis shops spread across Britain. Store managers and owners within this marketing group may choose to stock any or all of the wines recommended below.

 ## *White*

£3.00-3.50	● Londis Soave	*lightly honeyed fruit*	2
	Hugenot Hills South African		
	White	*pleasant simple wine*	2
	Sauvignon Blanc and Sauvignon-based wines		
£3.50-4.00	Londis VdP d'Oc Sauvignon		
	Blanc	*simple spicy fruit*	1
£4.00-4.50	Blossom Hill Californian		
	Sauvignon Blanc		1
	◆ La Fortuna Chilean Sauvignon		
	Blanc	*spicy*	1
	Cooks Sauvignon Blanc	*herby fruit*	1

Fuller-flavoured and fruity, but still relatively dry wines

£3.00 -3.50	Londis Hungarian Pinot		
	Nagyrede	*fresh with honey spice*	2
£3.50-4.00	Blossom Hill Californian White		2

| £4.00-4.50 | Jacob's Creek Australian Dry | | |
| | White | | 2 |

Chardonnay and Chardonnay blends

£3.00-3.50	Londis Hungarian Chardonnay		
	Nagyrede	*tropical citrus flavours*	2
£4.00-4.50	◆ Londis VdP d'Oc Chardonnay	*good buttery fruit*	2
	◆ Chapel Hill Hungarian Barrel		
	Aged Chardonnay	*attractive toasty fruit*	2
	◆ Lindemans Semillon/		
	Chardonnay	*lightly tropical with a good finish*	2
£4.50-5.00	Blossom Hill Californian		
	Chardonnay		2
	◆ Sutter Home Californian		
	Chardonnay	*lightly tropical fruit and apples*	2
	◆ Montana Marlborough New		
	Zealand Chardonnay	*full and fruity*	2
	Jacob's Creek Australian		
	Chardonnay		2
	◆ Lindemans Bin 65 Australian		
	Chardonnay	*oaky with tropical fruits*	2

Medium dry, very fruity wines to serve at any time

| £3.00-3.50 | Bulgarian Muscat/Ugni Blanc | 3 |

Sparkling wines for aperitifs and parties

£5.50-6.00	Orlando Carrington Brut	2
£6.00-6.50	Seaview Brut	2
£7.00-7.50	Lindauer New Zealand Brut	2

| £9.00-9.50 | ◆ Mumm Napa Cuvée Californian Sparkling Wine | | 2 |

Good wines for parties

| Under £3.00 | ● Londis VdP de l'Hérault Dry White | pleasant and easy-drinking | 2 |
| £3.50-4.00 | ◆ Stoneridge Australian Dry White | intensely tropical fruit | 2 |

Splashing out

| £5.00-5.50 | Orlando Australian Chardonnay | good fruit | 2 |
| | ◆ Gallo Turning Leaf Chardonnay | | 2 |

Red

Light and fruity wines for easy drinking at any time

£3.00-3.50	● Londis Valpolicella	easy-drinking
	Chapel Hill Hungarian Merlot	soft and fruity
£3.50-4.00	Londis Bardolino	easy-drinking
	Blossom Hill Californian Red	
	Stonebridge Australian Red	intense but dry summer fruits

Cabernet Sauvignon and Cabernet blends

| £3.00-3.50 | Chapel Hill Hungarian Cabernet Sauvignon | light and simple wine with raspberries |
| £3.50-4.00 | Londis VdP d'Oc Cabernet Sauvignon | simple fruit |

Medium-bodied wines to serve on their own or with food

£3.00-3.50	◆ Londis VdP d'Oc Merlot	*warm blackcurranty cedarwood fruit*
	Romanian Pinot Noir	
£3.50-4.00	Londis Chianti	*attractive fruit*
£4.50-5.00	◆ La Fortuna Chilean Merlot	*good fruit*

Cabernet Sauvignon and Cabernet blends

£3.00-3.50	Bulgarian Cabernet Sauvignon	
£3.50-4.00	Londis Claret	*attractive vegetal fruit*
£4.50-5.00	Blossom Hill Californian Cabernet Sauvignon	

Heavier wines to serve with food

Cabernet Sauvignon and Cabernet blends

£4.00-4.50	Jacob's Creek Australian Shiraz/Cabernet	
	◆ Lindemans Australian Shiraz/Cabernet	*full ripe blackcurrants*
	Lindemans Australian Cabernet Sauvignon	*full and fruity*

Good wines for parties

Under £3.00	● Londis VdP de l'Hérault Rouge	*warm easy-drinking fruit*
£3.00-3.50	● ◆ Londis Côtes du Rhône	*easy-drinking red berry fruit*

Splashing out

£5.00-5.50	Gallo Turning Leaf Caberney Sauvignon	*good fruit with fudge*

Mace

*T*here are 1200 stores in this marketing consortium and they are scattered accross the whole of the UK. They are individually owned or managed and may buy their wine from a number of sources. One of these is Booker Belmont Wholesale Limited who market their wines under the Malt House Vintner label (see page 78).

Majestic Wine Warehouses

*T*here are 58 Majestic Wine Warehouses scattered across central and southern England from East Anglia via Birmingham up to Stockport and Chester and as far as Bristol and Taunton in the West Country.

This company operates as a wholesaler so purchases must be a minimum of 12 bottles of wine, but you can mix your case and add odd bottles over the first 12. The wines are set out by country and wine growing region.

 White

Fresh and light wines for easy drinking at any time

£3.00-3.50 ◆ Domaine Le Puts Blanc VdP
des Côtes de Gascogne   *fresh herby apple fruit 2*

66

	Anjou Blanc Drouet Feres	*fresh almond fruit*	2
	Frascati Superiore Cantina Delle Torre		2
£3.50-4.00	Cortenova Trebbiano del Veneto Pasqua IT		1
	Pinot Grigio del Veneto Pasqua IT		1
£4.00-4.50	Domaines Felines Picpoul de Pinet	*distinctively fresh and spicy*	1
	◆ Soave Classico Tedeschi		2
£4.50-5.00	Marquès de Riscal Rueda Blanco	*interesting fresh fruit*	2

Sauvignon Blanc and Sauvignon blends

£3.00-3.50	Gyongyos Hungarian Sauvignon Blanc	*strong, minty and herbaceous*	1
£4.00-4.50	Sauvignon Blanc Fortant de France VdP d'Oc	*herbaceous with a touch of gooseberries*	1
£4.50-5.00	Santa Rita Chilean Reserve Sauvignon	*very fresh and minty*	1

Fuller-flavoured and fruity, but still relatively dry wines

£3.00-3.50	Carta Vieja Blanco	*unusual vanilla and almond fruit*	2
	Marquès de la Musa Dry White Conca de Barbera		2
£3.50-4.00	Kiesenhof South African Chenin Blanc	*minty apples and grapefruits*	2
£4.00-4.50	◆ Muscadet Sur Lie Château la Touche	*well balanced apples*	1

£4.50-5.00	◆ Vouvray Château de		
	Montfort	*delicious almost tropical fruit balanced with good acidity*	3
	Dry Muscat Joao Pires	*distinctive herby grapes*	3
	◆ Stoneleigh Riesling	*meadowsweet with good acidity*	2

Chardonnay and Chardonnay blends

£3.50-4.00	Chardonnay Atesino	*apples and spices with a touch of lemon and honey*	2
£4.00-4.50	Angoves Classic Reserve Australian Chardonnay	*oaky, lemony fruit*	2
	◆ Sutter Home Californian Chardonnay	*lightly tropical fruit and apples*	2
	◆ Lindemans Cawarra Colombard/Chardonnay	*lightly tropical with good finish*	2
	Kalinga Creek Semillon/ Chardonnay	*good depth of elegant tropical fruit*	2
£4.50-5.00	Carta Veija Antigua Chilean Chardonnay	*toasty oaky fruit*	2
	Bel Arbor Californian Chardonnay		
	◆ Kalinga Creek Chardonnay	*long tropical fruit*	2

Medium dry, very fruity wines to serve at any time

£3.50-4.00	Mosel Riesling	*minty grapefruit and flowers*	4
£4.00-4.50	◆ Jacob Zimmermann Kabinett Pfalz		4

Sparkling wines for aperitifs and parties

£5.00-5.50	Cava Brut Cristalino Jaume		
	Serra	*pleasantly fruity*	2
	Yaldara Australian Rosé	*pleasant berry fruit*	2
£7.50-8.00	Blanquette de Limoux Cuvée		
	Spéciale		1
	Seppelt Australian Chardonnay		
	Blanc de Blancs		1
◆	Taltarni Brut Tache Australian		
	Sparkling Wine		2

Dessert wine

£4.00-4.50	Jacob Zimmermann Spätlese	
	Pfalz	5

Good wines for parties

Under £3.00	Le St Cricq Blanc de Blancs	
	(Spanish wine; French bottled)	2
£3.00-3.50	Soave Torre Ora	2
£3.50-4.00	Misty Moorings Angoves White	2

Splashing out

£5.50-6.00	◆ Domaine des Salices Viognier	*attractive peachy fruit*	2
	◆ Chardonnay del Salento		
	Barrique	*long, full fruit and*	
		buttery wood	2
	◆ Reuilly	*elegant and long, minty*	
		gooseberry fruit	1

Red

Light and fruity wines for easy drinking at any time

£3.00-3.50	Valpolicella Torre Ora	*easy-drinking*
£3.50-4.00	Fortant de France Grenache VdP d'Oc	
	◆ Rosso Conero Umani Ronchi	*rich bramble and cherry fruit*
	Cante Cigale Rosé de Saignée VdP de l'Hérault	*easy-drinking rose petals and pears*
	Carta Vieja Chilean Merlot	*fresh and easy red berry fruit*
£3.50-4.00	◆ Domaine St-Jean Côtes du Roussillon	*attractively ripe fruit*
£4.00-4.50	Valpolicella Classico Tedeschi	
	◆ Dolcetto d'Alba	*easy-drinking sweet ripe fruit*

Cabernet Sauvingon and Cabernet blends

	◆ Cabernet Sauvignon VdP de la Haute Vallée de l'Aude	*fresh berry fruit*

Medium-bodied wines to serve on their own or with food

£3.00-3.50	Syrah Sica Limouxins VdP de la Haute Vallée de l'Aude	*warm fruit cake and raisins*
	Marquès de la Musa Red Conca de Barbera	
£3.50-4.00	Chianti Grati	*full flowery fruit with violets*

	Vina Azabache Rioja Tinto	*hot ripe raspberries and blackberries*
£4.00-4.50	Domaine des Murettes Minervois	*hot vegetal fruit with coffee flavours*
	Fitou Les Producteurs de Paziols	*attractive warm flowery fruit*
	Montepulciano d'Abruzzo Barone Cornacchia	*full-bodied style*
	Vina Azabache Garnacha	*long blackberries and plums*
	◆ Kiesenhof Pinotage Paarl	*attractive ripe fruit*
	Waimanu New Zealand Premium Dry Red	*flowery blackcurrants with light vanilla oak*
£4.50-5.00	Domaine de la Baranière Côtes du Rhône	*hot berry fruit*
	◆ Château Quartironi de Sars St Chinian	
	◆ Guelbenzu Jardin Navarra Spanish Red	*well balanced bramble and plum fruit, long and deep*
	◆ Bel Arbor Californian Merlot	*good depth of rich plummy fruit with a touch of oak*

Cabernet Sauvignon and Cabernet blends

£3,00-3.50	Cabernet Sauvingon VdP de l'Aude	
£3.50-4.00	◆ Claret Yves Barry	*simple but attractive fruit with cedarwood*
£4.00-4.50	Undurraga Chilean Cabernet Sauvignon	

	◆ Lindemans Cawarra Shiraz/ Cabernet	*full and ripe blackcurrant fruit*
£4.50-5.00	◆ Oaky Claret Raoul Johnston	*well balanced fruit, oak and tannin*
	Santa Rita Reserva Chilean Cabernet	*good depth of ripe fruit with black treacle*
	◆ Bel Arbor Californian Cabernet Sauvignon	*ripe red berry fruit with good length*

Heavier wines to serve with food

£3.50-4.00	Gran Dolfos Bodegas Farina Spanish Red	
	Carta Vieja Tinto Chilean Red	*ripe blackcurrants*
£4.00-4.50	Negroamaro del Salento	*Distinctive raisin fruit and Christmas cake*
	◆ José d Sousa JM da Fonseca	*rich and long vegetal fruit*
	◆ Sangre de Toro Spanish Red	*full ripe fruit*
	Bright Brothers Estremadura	*plums and berry fruit with chocolate and oak*
	Kalinga Creek Cabernet	*rich leathery fruit*
£4.50-5.00	Notarpanaro Taurino	*distinctive almonds and raisin fruit*
	◆ Marquès de Grinon Rioja	*ripe vegetal fruit*
	◆ Lindemans Bin 50 Shiraz	*massive berry fruit with leathery tones*
	Angoves Classic Reserve Shiraz	*easy ripe vegetal fruit with liquorice*

Good wines for parties

£3.00-3.50	Cabernet Sauvignon VdP du Gard	*soft milky fruit*
	Montepulciano d'Abruzzo Sole	*sweet flowery fruit*
	Cortenova Merlot, Grave del Friuli Pasqua	
£3.50-4.00	Sutter Home Californian Red	

Splashing out

£5.50-6.00	◆ Guelbenzu Navarra	*blackcurrants and cedarwood*
£6.50-7.00	Mas des Bressades Costières de Nîmes	*full fruit, coffee and tar*

Makro

*T*here are 26 Makro stores scattered across the UK. They supply a variety of small grocers, caterers and individuals.

White

Fresh and light wines for easy drinking at any time

£3.00-3.50	Servus Australian White Wine		2
£3.50-4.00	VdP de Gascogne		2
£4.00-4.50	Bianco di Custoza		2
	Pinot Grigio Ca Donini		2
	Marquès de Caceras White Rioja	*fresh with reasonable fruit*	2
	Torres Vina Sol	*fresh and fruity*	2

Sauvignon Blanc and Sauvignon-based wines

£3.50-4.00	Sauvignon VdP d'Oc		1
£4.50-5.00	◆ Montana Marlborough New Zealand Sauvignon Blanc	*spicy herbaceous fruit*	1

Fuller-flavoured and fruity, but still relatively dry wines

£3.50-4.00	Angove's Misty Moorings Australian White	*good fruit*	2

Chardonnay and Chardonnay blends

£3.50-4.00	Butterfly Ridge Australian Colombard/Chardonnay		2
£4.00-4.50	Chardonnay delle Tre Venezie Ca Donini		2
	◆ Sutter Home Californian Chardonnay	*lightly tropical fruity with apples*	2
	Jacob's Creek Australian Semillon/Chardonnay		
	◆ Montana Marlborough New Zealand Chardonnay	*full and fruity*	2

Sparkling wines for aperitifs and parties

£5.50-6.00	Asti Martini Brut	2
	Asti Spumante Martini	7
£6.50-7.00	Lindauer New Zealand Brut	2

Good wines for parties

£3.00-3.50	Castello di Liria Spanish Dry White	2
	Blossom Hill California White	2

Splashing out

£5.50-6.00	◆ Rosemount Australian Chardonnay	*full tropical fruit*	2

Red

Light and fruity wines for easy drinking at any time

Under £3.00	Valpolicella
£3.00-3.50	Blossom Hill Californian Red
£4.00-4.50	Sutter Home Californian Zinfandel

Medium-bodied wines to serve on their own or with food

Cabernet Sauvignon and Cabernet blends

£3.00-3.50	Fitou
£3.50-4.00	Butterfly Ridge Australian Shiraz/ Cabernet

Heavier wines to serve with food

£4.50-5.00	Torres Coronas Penedès Spanish Red

Cabernet Sauvignon and Cabernet blends

£4.00-4.50	Jacob's Creek Australian Shiraz/ Cabernet

Good wines for parties

£3.00-3.50 ● Castello di Liria Spanish Red   *easy-drinking*

Splashing out

£5.50-6.00   Roo's Leap Australian
Shiraz/Cabernet
Wolf Blass Australian
Shiraz/Cabernet
£6.00-6.50   ◆ Rosemount Australian Shiraz

Malt House Vintners

*T*his is one of the retail outlets for the wines of Booker Belmont Wholesale Limited. There are over 100 Malt House Vintner shops scattered across the UK. These wines are also available in some Mace grocers shops.

 White

Fresh and light wines for easy drinking at any time

£3.00-3.50	Minervois Blanc		1
£3.50-4.00	Domaine au Late VdP des		
	Côtes de Gascogne	*fresh and fruity*	2
£4.50-5.00	Château Queyret-Pouillac		
	Entre-deux-Mers	*fresh and fruity*	2

Sauvignon Blanc and Sauvignon blends

£3.50-4.00	Bordeaux Sauvignon	*light gooseberry fruit*	1

Fuller-flavoured and fruity, but still relatively dry wines

£3.50-4.00	Australian Semillon	*pineapple fruit with a touch of oak*	2
£4.00-4.50	New Zealand Dry White		2

Chardonnay and Chardonnay blends

£4.50-5.00	Beaujolais Blanc Chardonnay		
	Le Magny		2
	Australian Chardonnay	*tropical fruits with oak*	2

Medium dry, very fruity wines to serve at any time

Under £3.00   Obermeister Liebfraumilch   4

Sparkling wines for aperitifs and parties

£4.50-5.00   ◆ Asti Italian Sparkling Wine   *fresh grapey fruit*   7

Splashing out

£6.50-7.00   Pouilly Fumé   *smoky gooseberry*
                                                                      fruit   1

 Red

Light and fruity wines for easy drinking at any time

£3.00-3.50   Rosé d'Anjou   *sweet fruit*
                   South African Red Wine
£3.50-4.00   South African Pinotage

Medium-bodied wines to serve on their own or with food

£4.50-5.00   Côtes du Rhône   *fresh and fruity*
                   Villa Cerna Chianti Classico
                   Cabernet Sauvignon and Cabernet blends
£3.50-4.00   Chilean Cabernet Sauvignon   *rich blackcurrant fruit*
£4.00-4.50   Château des Bruges Bordeaux
                        Rouge
£4.50-5.00   Malt House Vintners Australian
                        Cabernet Sauvignon

BEST WINE BUYS

Heavier wines to serve with food

£4.50-5.00 ◆ Valdepeñas Reserva *good vegetal fruit*

Good wines for parties

£3.00-3.50 Malt House Vintners French
Vin Rouge

Splashing out

£5.50-6.00 St Emilion *soft mature fruit*
£6.00-6.50 ◆ Crozes Hermitage *well concentrated fruit*

Marks & Spencer

*T*here are 283 Marks & Spencer stores scattered across the country with branches in England, Scotland, Wales and Northern Ireland. The wines are arranged by country and then by wine regions within those countries.

White

Fresh and light wines for easy drinking at any time

£3.00-3.50	VdP du Gers	*easy-drinking fruit*	2
£3.50-4.00	◆ VdP des Côtes de Gascogne		
	Plaimont	*attractive fresh fruit*	2
	Bianco di Puglia	*apple fresh*	1
£4.00-4.50	Vermentino VdP d'Oc		
	Domaines Virginie	*attractive spicy fruit*	2
	Pinot Grigio delle Tre Venezie		
	Vino de Tavola	*fresh almond fruit*	2
	Frascati Superiore Pallavacini	*fresh spicy fruit with good length*	2
£4.50-5.00	◆ Vouvray Domaine Pouvraie	*lemons and almonds*	3

Sauvignon Blanc and Sauvignon blends

£4.00-4.50	Lontue Chilean Sauvignon Blanc	*good fruit*	1
£4.50-5.00	Madeba Reserve South African Sauvignon Blanc	*minty gooseberry fruit*	1
	◆ Kaituna Hills New Zealand Sauvignon Blanc	*strong minty gooseberry fruit*	1

Fuller-flavoured and fruity, but still relatively dry wines

£3.50-4.00	Cape Country Colombard KWV		2
£4.00-4.50	Roussanne VdP d'Oc Domaines Virginie	*interesting spicy fruit*	2
	◆ Malvasia del Salento	*distinctive spicy fruit with citrus finish*	2
£4.50-5.00	◆ Voignier Domaine de Mandeville VdP d'Oc	*fresh with a touch of peaches*	2

Chardonnay and Chardonnay blends

£4.00-4.50	◆ Chardonnay Domaine de Mandeville VdP d'Oc	*excellent depth of lightly tropical fruit*	2
	Chardonnay delle Tre Venezie	*pears and candy*	2
	Casa Leona Chilean Chardonnay	*lush pineapple*	2
£4.50-5.00	Gold Label Chardonnay VdP d'Oc Domaines Virginie	*good fruit*	2
	White Burgundy Cave de Lugny	*good length with citrus fruits*	2
	◆ Lontue Chilean Chardonnay Vina San Pedro	*rich tropical fruit*	2
	◆ Semillon/Chardonnay Bin 501	*easy-drinking tropical fruit*	2
	◆ Honey Tree Semillon/Chardonnay	*very attractive well balanced fruit and oak*	2
	Kaituna Hills New Zealand Chardonnay	*elegantly fruity*	2

Medium dry, very fruity wines to serve at any time

£4.00-4.50	Australian Medium Dry		
	Lindemans	*easy-drinking*	3
	Niersteiner Spiegelberg		
	Kabinett	*pleasant flowery*	
		grapefruit fruit	4
£4.50-5.00	Zell Castle Riesling Spätlese		
	Klosterhof	*fresh and attractive*	
		fruit	5

Sparkling wines for aperitifs and parties

£5.00-5.50	Malvasia Prosecco Italian		
	Sparkling Wine	*easy-drinking grapey*	
		fruit	5
	Cava Segura Viudas	*good fruit*	2
£6.00-6.50	French Sparkling		
	Chardonnay		2
	◆ Crémant de Bougogne Cave		
	de Lugny		2
£7.00-7.50	◆ Bluff Hill New Zealand		
	Sparkling Wine Montana	*fruity*	2

Good wines for parties

£3.00-3.50	◆ Conca de Barbera Spanish		
	White	*fresh and fruity*	2
£3.50-4.00	Bellaura Bianco di Sicilia	*easy-drinking apples*	
		and honey	2

Splashing out

£6.00-6.50	◆ Jeunes Vignes La Chablisiènne	*steely fruit with honey* 2
£7.00-7.50	◆ Chardonnay Hunter Valley Rosemount Estate	*elegant, well balanced oak and fruit* 2
	◆ Saints Gisborne Chardonnay Montana	*excellent balance of toasty buttery fruit and oak* 2
£8.00-8.50	◆ Chablis La Chablisiènne	*good depth of fruit* 2

Red

Light and fruity wines for easy drinking at any time

£3.00-3.50	Merlot del Veneto	*easy-drinking and attractive fruit*
£4.00-4.50	◆ Merlot Domaine de Mandeville VdP d'Oc	*good depth of berry bramble fruit*
	◆ Merlot VdP d'Oc Domaines Virginie	*blackcurrant and soft bramble fruit*
	Barbera del Piemonte Girodano Uruguayan Merlot/Tannat	*soft easy-drinking fruit*

Medium-bodied wines to serve on their own or with food

£3.50-4.00	Montepulciano d'Abruzzo	*good depth of warm fruit*
£4.00- 4.50	Fitou	*good fruit*

	Chinon Caves des Vins de Rabelais	*particularly fruity*
	Domaine St Germain Minervois	*attractive soft fruit*
	Portan VdP d'Oc Domaines Virginie	*good plums and bramble fruit*
	◆ Rioja Bodegas AGE	*new style fruity wine*
	Penascal Vino de Mesa Tinto Spanish Red	*distinctive orange fruit*
£4.50-5.00	◆ Australian Shiraz Penfolds	*easy-drinking with good depth of fruit*

Cabernet Sauvignon and Cabernet blends

£3.00-3.50	◆ Cabernet Sauvignon Svischtov Region	*mature ripe vegetal fruit*
£4.00-4.50	◆ Gold Medal Cabernet Sauvignon VdP d'Oc	*good depth ripe blackcurrant fruit*
	Trapiche Argentinian Cabernet Sauvignon/Malbec	*easy-drinking fruit*
£4.50-5.00	Château Cazeau Classic Claret Bordeaux	*long easy-drinking fruit*
	◆ Central Chilean Valley Cabernet Sauvignon	*long blackcurrant fruit*

Heavier wines to serve with food

3.50-4.00	◆ Rosso di Puglia Italian Red	*rich cakey fruit with great depth*
£4.00-4.50	◆ Domaine Belle Feuille Côtes du Rhône	*delicious depth of rich berry fruit with plums and chocolate*

£4.50-5.00 ◆ Trapiche Argentinian
Malbec Oak Cask Reserve *juicy fruit with oak*

Cabernet Sauvignon and Cabernet blends

£4.50-5.00 ◆ Australian Shiraz/Cabernet
Bin 505 *lush and juicy berry fruit*
Honey Tree Shiraz/Cabernet *warm juicy fruit with toasty finish*

Good wines for parties

£3.00-3.50 Domaine St Pierre VdP de
l'Hérault *easy-drinking cherry fruit*

£3.50-4.00 Cardillo Rosso di Sicilia *easy-drinking slightly warm fruit*

£4.00-4.50 Australian Red Pheasant
Gully Shiraz *fruity and easy-drinking*

Splashing out

£5.00-5.50 Bordeaux Matured in Oak *particularly toasty*

£5.50-6.00 ◆ Gran Calesa Costers del
Segre Spanish Red *ripe vegetal fruit*
◆ Maipo Cabernet Sauvignon
Reserve *deep blackcurrant fruit*

Morrisons

*T*here are now 87 Morrisons stores scattered across the whole of the North East, North West and the Midlands as far south as Shrewsbury and Walsall. The wines are arranged by country and wine growing region.

 White

Fresh and light wines for easy drinking at any time

Under £3.00	Anjou Blanc Vincent de Valloire	*fresh almond fruit with a touch of honey*	2
	● Trebbiano del Vigneti del Sol Italian White		2
£3.00-3.50	VdP des Côtes de Gascogne	*particularly fruity*	2
	◆ Winter Hill VdP d'Oc	*attractive, fresh and easy-drinking*	1
	Terres Noires Picpoul	*fresh and easy-drinking*	1
	Orvieto Classico	*fresh and long with honey and almonds*	2
£4.00-4.50	Laperouse VdP d'Oc		2
	Torres Vina Sol	*fresh and fruity*	2
£4.50-5.00	◆ Château Saint Gallier Graves	*very good fruit*	2

Sauvignon Blanc and Sauvignon-based wines

| **Under £3.00** | Romanian Classic Sauvignon Blanc | | 1 |
| **£3.00-3.50** | Bordeaux Sauvignon Blanc | *easy-drinking* | 2 |

	◆ Val de Zaro Chilean Sauvignon Blanc	*very good ripe fruit*	1
£3.50-4.00	Gato Blanco Chilean Sauvignon Blanc	*good spicy fruit*	1

Fuller-flavoured and fruity, but still relatively dry wines

Under £3.00	Bulgarian Country White		4
	Chapel Hill Ursai Oliver	*distinctively aromatic*	2
£3.00-3.50	◆ St Ursula Devils Rock Riesling	*fresh and grapefruity*	2
£4.00-4.50	Timara New Zealand White	*minty fruit*	1

Chardonnay and Chardonnay blends

Under £3.00	Bear Ridge Chardonnay	*fresh and spicy*	2
£3.00-3.50	La Source Chardonnay VdP d'Oc		2
	◆ Chapel Hill Chardonnay	*full and fruity with citrus fruits*	2
£3.50-4.00	Chais Cuxac Chardonnay		2
	Coldridge Australian Chenin/ Chardonnay	*fresh tropical fruit*	2
£4.00-4.50	◆ Glenn Ellen Californian Chardonnay	*particularly fruity*	2
	◆ Barramundi Australian Semillon/Chardonnay	*fresh and tropical with a touch of oak*	2
£4.50-5.00	◆ Cooks New Zealand Chardonnay	*full tropical fruit*	2
	◆ Penfolds Bin 21 Australian Semillon/Chardonnay	*good tropical fruit*	2
	◆ Lindemans Bin 65 Australian Chardonnay	*lightly oaked tropical fruits*	2

Medium dry, very fruity wines to serve at any time

Under £3.00	Flonheimer Adelberg Kabinett	*easy-drinking*	4
£3.00-3.50	Franz Reh Kabinett Niersteiner		4
£3.50-4.00	◆ Franz Reh Spätlese	*rich raisiny fruit*	5
	Wiltinger Scharzberg Spätlese	*particularly fruity*	4

Sparkling wines for aperitifs and parties

£4.50-5.00	Asti Gianni Italian Sparkling Wine		7
	◆ Cristalino Brut Spanish Cava	*particularly fruity*	1
£5.00-5.50	◆ Barramundi Australian Sparkling Wine	*very good fruit*	2
	Seppelt Great Western Australian Brut		2
£5.50-6.00	Freixenet Brut Rosé Spanish Cava		2
£6.00-6.50	Asti Martini Italian Sparkling Wine		7
	Seaview Australian Brut		2
£6.50-7.00	Gratien & Meyer Brut		2

Dessert wine

£3.00-3.50	Moscatel de Valencia	8

Good wines for parties

Under £3.00	Gabbia D'Oro Italian Vino Bianco		3
£3.00-3.50	Côtes du Roussillon Blanc	*easy-drinking*	2

Fair Cape South African
Chenin Blanc *fresh and easy-drinking* 2

Splashing out

£6.00-6.50 ◆ Wolf Blass Australian
Chardonnay *full and fruity* 2

£9.00-9.50 ◆ Nicole d'Aurigny Champagne 1

Red

Light and fruity wines for easy drinking at any time

Under £3.00   Le Cellier La Chouf Minervois

    ● Merlot Vigneti del Sole
       Italian Red

    ◆ Romanian Classic Pinot
       Noir Dealul Mare Region *mature fruit*

£3.00-3.50 ◆ La Source Merlot VdP d'Oc *good depth of strawberry fruit*

      La Source Syrah Rosé
      VdP d'Oc *pretty berry fruit*

      Côtes du Ventoux

    ◆ Montepulciano d'Abruzzo *good fruit*

      Fair Cape South African
      Cinsault

£3.50-4.00 ◆ Château Jourgrand St Chinian *fresh cherry fruit*

Medium-bodied wines to serve on their own or with food

Under £3.00   Les Fenouillets Corbières

£3.00-3.50	Côtes du Roussillon Villages	
	Coteaux du Languedoc	*easy long fruit*
● ◆	Chianti Uggiano	*fresh cherry and violet fruit*
◆	Val Longa Portuguese Red	*fresh, full and fruity*
	Romanian Special Reserve Pinot Noir	*long vegetal fruit*
	Valdezaro Chilean Red	*easy-drinking*
£3.50-4.00 ◆	Uggiano Chianti Classico	
	Morrisons Rioja	
	Côtes du Buzet	*particularly fruity*
	Blossom Hill Californian Red	
	Jacob's Creek Australian Red	
£4.00-4.50	Solana Cencibel Valdepeñas Spanish Red	*fresh and fruity*
◆	Glen Ellen Californian Merlot	*soft blackcurrants and bramble fruit*

Cabernet Sauvignon and Cabernet blends

Under £3.00 ●	Bulgarian Cabernet Sauvignon	
£3.00-3.50	Cabernet Sauvignon VdP d'Oc	
	Val de Zaro Chilean Cabernet Sauvignon	*easy jammy fruit*
£3.50-4.00	Morrisons Claret	
◆	Chais Cuxac VdP d'Oc Cabernet Sauvignon	*particularly fruity*
◆	Coldridge Australian Shiraz/ Cabernet	*particularly fruity and easy-drinking*
£4.50-5.00	Château Saint Gallier Graves	*good fruit and tannins*

Heavier wines to serve with food

| Under £3.00 | Soveral Portuguese Red | |
| | Moroccan Red | |

91

£4.00-4.50	Barramundi Shiraz/Merlot	*attractive mellow fruit*
£4.50-5.00	Torres Sangredetoro Spanish Red	*distinctive*

Cabernet and Cabernet blends

£3.00-3.50	Romanian Cabernet	*distinctive*
£4.50-5.00	Hanwood Estate Cabernet Sauvignon	*particularly fruity*
	Lindemans Australian Cabernet Sauvignon	*full and fruity*

Good wines for parties

£3.00-3.50	◆ Winter Hill VdP de l'Aude	*easy-drinking summer berry fruit*
	Chapel Hill Cabernet Sauvignon	*light and simple wine with raspberries*
	VdP d'Oc Merlot	*particularly fruity*

Oddbins

*T*here are 215 outlets in this chain of adventurous wine shops covering the country from Inverness to Plymouth. The wines are set out by country and by wine region.

White

£3.00-3.50	Cuvée de Grignon VdP de l'Aude		2
	Santara Spanish Dry White	*attractively fresh and fruity*	2
£3.50-4.00	Oddbins White VdP des Côtes de Gascogne		2
	VdP d'Oc Terret Lurton	*apple fresh*	1
	Puglian White	*spicy fruit*	2
	La Cata Blanca Spanish White	*attractive apples and pears*	2
£4.00-4.50	Domaine de Joy VdP des Côtes de Gascogne	*fresh and fruity with grapefruit and pears*	2
£4.50-5.00	Muscadet Domaine de la Grange		1
	◆ Greco di Puglia	*fresh with good depth of fruit*	2

Sauvignon Blanc and Sauvignon blends

£4.00-4.50	Domaine des Salices Sauvignon Lurton	*minty gooseberries*	1
	Marquès de Grinon Durius Spanish White	*minty and herbaceous*	1
◆	Andes Peak Chilean Sauvignon Blanc	*easy-drinking minty fresh apples*	1
	Villa Montes Chilean Sauvignon Blanc Curico Valley	*herby limes*	1
£4.50-5.00	Sauvignon Rueda	*particularly fruity*	1
	Montana Marlborough New Zealand Sauvignon Blanc	*spicy herbaceous fruit*	1

Fuller-flavoured and fruity, but still relatively dry wines

£3.00-3.50	Chapel Hill Hungarian Irsai Oliver	*distinctively aromatic fruit with grapes*	2
	Chapel Hill Hungarian Rhine Riesling		3
	Nagyrede Hungarian Dry Muscat	*distinctively fruity*	2
	Eden Valley Estates Australian Riesling	*particularly fruity*	4
£4.00-4.50 ◆	Cono Sur Chilean Gewürztraminer	*fresh flowery lychees*	2
	Penfolds Bin 202 Australian Riesling	*distinctive citrus fruits and flowers*	2
£4.50-5.00	Peter Lehmann Australian Semillon	*tropical citrus fruit with a touch of oak*	2

	◆ Wynn's Koonawarra Rhine Riesling	*fresh grapefruit* 3

Chardonnay and Chardonnay blends

£3.00-3.50	Bulgarian Khan Krum Reserve Chardonnay	*oaky* 2
£3.50-4.00	◆ Chapel Hill Hungarian Oaked Chardonnay	*lightly tropical* 2
£4.00-4.50	Santara Spanish Chardonnay	*particularly fruity* 2
	◆ Andes Peak Chilean Chardonnay	*lush pineapple fruit* 2
	◆ Lindemans Australian Colombard/Chardonnay	*lightly tropical with a good finish* 2
	Jacob's Creek Australian Semillon/Chardonnay	2
£4.50-5.00	◆ James Herrick Chardonnay VdP d'Oc	*full and fruity with oak* 2
	◆ Italian Chardonnay del Salento 'Le Trulle'	*attractive* 2
	Springfield South African Chardonnay	*good fruit* 2
	◆ Redwood Trail Californian Chardonnay	*toasty oaky fruit* 2
	◆ Santa Carolina Chilean Chardonnay	*particularly fruity* 2
	◆ Caliterra Casablanca Valley Chilean Chardonnay	*very fresh tropical citrus fruits* 2
	◆ Lindemans Bin 65 Australian Chardonnay	*lightly oaked tropical fruits* 2

Medium dry, very fruity wines to serve at any time

£3.50-4.00	Bereich Bernkastel St Ursula	4

Sparkling wines for aperitifs and parties

£5.50-6.00	Segura Viudas Reserva Spanish Cava	1
£6.00-6.50	Seaview Australian Brut	2
£7.00-7.50	Crémant de Bourgogne Caves Lugny	2
	Montana Lindauer New Zealand Brut	2
£7.50-8.00	◆ Seaview Australian Pinot/ Chardonnay	2

Good wines for parties

£3.00-3.50	Chardonnay Vino da Tavola Casona	*easy-drinking*	2
£3.50-4.00	◆ Nagyrede Hungarian Pinot Gris	*good depth of lightly spicy fruit*	2

Splashing out

£6.00-6.50	◆ Rothbury Estate Barrel-Fermented Chardonnay	*oaky fruit*	2
£7.00-7.50	◆ Richard Hamilton Australian Chardonnay	*tropical pineapple and oak*	2

Red and rosé

Light and fruity wines for easy drinking at any time

Under £3.00	Riva Sangiovese di Romagna	
£3.00-3.50	Château de Jau VdP des Côtes Catalanes	*particularly fruity*
	Côtes du Roussillon JeanJean	
£3.50-4.00	Côtes du Ventoux Les Cailloux	
	Chapel Hill Hungarian Kekfrankos	*juicy fruit*
	Bulgarian Gamza Reserve Suhindol	*good fruit*
£4.00-4.50	Santa Rita Chilean Cabernet Sauvignon Rosé	
£4.50-5.00	Peter Lehmann Australian Grenache	*easy-drinking summer berries*

Medium-bodied wines to serve on their own or with food

£3.00-3.50	Domaine de la Grange VdP du Vallée de Paradis	
	Merlot Reserves Suhindol Region	*fruity*
£3.50-4.00	Côtes du Rhônes Enclave des Papes	
	Domaine d'Abrens Minervois Jeanjean	
	Puglian Red	*full raisiny fruit*
	Valley Estates Australian Dry Red	

£4.00-4.50	Château Lartigue Côtes de Castillon	*attractive red berries and fudge*
	Barton & Gustier Merlot	*easy-drinking full fruit*
	◆ Orbio Rioja Tempranillo	*attractive easy-drinking fruit*
£4.50-5.00	James Herrick Cuvée Simone VdP d'Oc	*rich spicy vegetal fruit*
	◆ Domaine de Mas Carlot Costière de Nîmes	*good blackcurrant and raspberry fruit*
	Fuente del Ritmo La Mancha Spanish Tempranillo	*cherry fruit with oak*
	◆ Redwood Trail Californian Pinot Noir	*warm vegetal fruit with good length*

Cabernet Sauvignon and Cabernet blends

£3.00-3.50	Bulgarian Cabernet Sauvignon Suhindol	
£3.50-4.00	Palacio de la Vega Tempranillo Joven	
	Rauli Chilean Cabernet/Merlot Maipo	
£4.00-4.50	VdP d'Oc Cabernet Sauvignon	
£4.50-5.00	◆ Redwood Trail Cabernet Sauvignon	*ripe vegetal plums with good length*

Heavier wines to serve with food

£4.00-4.50	Albor Campo Veijo Rioja	
	Balbi Vineyard Argentinian Malbec	*rich berry fruit*

£4.50-5.00	Châteaux de Lascaux Coteaux	
	du Languedoc	*full and fruity with warm tannin*
	Palacio de la Vega Crianza	
	Navarra	*rich vegetal fruit with vanilla*
◆	Peter Lehmann Vine Vale	
	Australian Shiraz	*rich leathery fruit*

Cabernet Sauvignon and Cabernet blends

£3.50-4.00	Glenloth Australian Shiraz/	
	Cabernet	
£4.00-4.50	Primitivo del Salento	*ripe and chocolately*
	Palacio de la Vega Navarra	
	Cabernet Sauvignon/	
	Tempranillo	*long and full-bodied*
◆	Lindemans Cawarra Australian	
	Shiraz/Cabernet	*full ripe blackcurrant fruit*
	Orlando Jacob's Creek Australian	
	Shiraz/Cabernet	
◆	Penfolds Rawson's Retreat	
	Shiraz/Cabernet	*long blackcurrant fruit*

Good wines for parties

£3.00-3.50	Santara Spanish Dry Red	*easy-drinking and fruity*
	Cuvée de Grignon VdP de	
	l'Aude	*easy fudgy fruit*

Splashing out

£6.50-7.00	◆ Vacqueyras Cabassol	*rich and spicy*
	Hauts Côtes de Beaune Tete	
	de Cuvée	*attractive vegetal fruit*

Pioneer Stores

*T*his chain of stores is part of Co-operative Retail Services and stocks a similar range of wines to Leo's (see page 55).

Presto

*T*he are around 170 stores in this group of small supermarkets. Their wines are serviced by their sister chain Safeway (see below).

 # Safeway

 *T*his supermarket chain has 375 stores covering the whole of the mainland of Great Britain. Wines are set out in two sections, red and white, and within these sections by country and wine growing region. Many, though not all these wines can also be found in Presto stores.

 ## White

£3.00-3.50	Safeway Côtes du Luberon Ryman	*fresh and fruity*	2
	Safeway Sicilian Dry White		2
	Vina Malea Oaked Viura Vino de la Tierrs Manchuela	*attractive honeyed fruit lightly oaked*	2
	Safeway South African Colombard Robertson		1
£3.50-4.00	Domaine du Rey VdP des Côtes de Gascogne	*easy-drinking fruit*	2
£4.00-4.50	◆ Safeway Oak-aged Bordeaux Blanc	*fresh and well balanced*	2
	Laperouse VdP d'Oc	*interesting fruit*	2
	Zagara Grillo Vino da Tavola di Sicillia	*toasty almond fruit with a touch of honey*	2

	Safeway Orvieto Classico		
	Secco	*particularly fruity*	2
£4.50-5.00	Vieux Manoir de Maransan		
	Côtes du Rhône	*attractively fruity*	2

Sauvignon Blanc and Sauvignon blends

£3.00-3.50	Hungarian Sauvignon Blanc		
	River Duna	*soft gooseberry fruit*	1
£3.50-4.00	Safeway Bergerac Sauvignon	*particularly fruity*	1
£4.00-4.50	◆ Château de Plantier		
	Entre-deux-Mers	*particularly fruity*	1
	◆ River Duna Sauvignon Blanc		
	Special Cuvée	*fresh but ripe gooseberry fruit with herbs*	1
£4.50-5.00	◆ Casablanca White Label		
	Chilean Sauvignon Blanc	*ripe easy-drinking fruit*	1
	◆ Breakaway Australian		
	Sauvignon/Semillon	*attractive full-flavoured fruit*	2

Fuller-flavoured and fruity, but still relatively dry wines

£3.00-3.50	Safeway Hungarian Dry		
	Muscat Nagyrede	*distinctively fruity*	2
	River Duna Irsai Oliver	*fresh spicy, herby fruit*	2
	Rikat Special Selection		
	Rousse	*well balanced lightly oaked*	2
£3.50-4.00	Almond Grove Riesling Dry		
	Pfalz	*attractively grapefruity*	2
	Safeway Australian Dry White		2
	◆ H.G.Brown Bin No 6 Australian		
	Oaked Colombard	*oaky buttery fruit*	2

| £4.50-5.00 | Château Haut Bonfils Barrel-
Fermented Bordeaux
Semillon | *very oaky* | 2 |

Chardonnay and Chardonnay blends

£3.00-3.50	Quagga South African Colombard/Chardonnay		2
£3.50-4.00	◆ Chardonnay VdP du Jardin de la France	*good value easy- drinking wine*	2
	◆ Kirkwood Moldovan Chardonnay	*lightly oaked fruit*	2
	Bulgarian Chardonnay Reserve Russe	*easy-drinking lightly oaked*	2
£4.00-4.50	H.D.Ryman Chardonny VdP d'Oc	*buttery fruit*	2
	Somontano Spanish Chardonnay	*soft vegetal and toasty*	2
	Caliterra Chilean Chardonnay Curico	*tropical citrus fruits*	2
	Monty's Hill Chardonnay/ Colombard	*lightly tropical citrus fruits*	
	◆ Safeway Semillon/Chardonnay SE. Australia	*good lightly tropical fruit*	2
£4.50-5.00	◆ Domaine de Rivoyre Chardonnay VdP d'Oc	*fresh and tropical*	2
	Terre Vivante Chardonnay/ Viognier Oaked	*spicy apricots and tangerines*	2
	◆ Chapel Hill Barrique-Fermented Chardonnay	*attractively tropical and toasty*	2

	Safeway Australian		
	Chardonnay	*good tropical fruit*	2
◆	Hardy's Private Bin Oaked		
	Australian Chardonnay	*attractive lightly tropical fruit*	2
◆	Hardy's Nottage Hill Australian		
	Chardonnay	*easy-drinking tropical fruit with oak*	2

Medium dry, very fruity wines to serve at any time

Under £3.00	Safeway Bulgarian Country	
	Wine Russe	4
£3.50-4.00	Safeway Kabinett Rheinpfalz	4

Sparkling wines for aperitifs and parties

£5.00-5.50	◆ Safeway Spanish Cava	*fresh and fruity with just a little earthiness*	1
£5.50-6.00	◆ Safeway Chardonnay Italian		
	Spumante Brut	*easy-drinking*	1
£6.00-6.50	Asti Martini Italian Sparkling		
	Wine		7
	Safeway Saumur		1
£7.00-7.50	Safeway Crémant de		
	Bourgogne Brut		2
	Le Grand Pavillon de Boschendal		
	Cuvée South African Brut		1
	Lindauer New Zealand Brut		2

Good wines for parties

Under £3.00	Safeway Hungarian Country Wine		2
£3.00-3.50	Italian Bianco di Verona	*soft easy-drinking wine*	2
£3.50-4.00	La Coume de Peyre VdP des Côtes de Gascogne	*fresh and fruity*	2

Splashing out

£6.00-6.50	◆ Cune Monopole Barrel-Fermented Rioja	*oaky with good fruit*	2
	◆ Hunter Valley Chardonnay Rosemount	*good tropical fruit*	2
£7.50-8.00	Safeway Chablis Cuvée Dom Yveon Pautre	*good steely fruit*	1

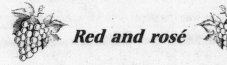

Red and rosé

Light and fruity wines for easy drinking at any time

Under £3.00	Bulgarian Country Wine Pinot and Merlot Sliven Region	
£3.00-3.50	Safeway Côtes du Ventoux	*particularly fruity*
	Merlot VdP des Coteaux de l'Ardèche	
	Côtes de Luberon Rosé	*good fruit*
	Safeway VdP de Vaucluse	*easy-drinking*
	Italian Rosso di Verona	*attractive easy-drinking*
	Tocornal Chilean Red	
£3.50-4.00	Safeway Côtes du Roussillon Villages	*easy-drinking*

	◆ Safeway Bergerac	
	Vina Albali Spanish	
	Tempranillo	*fresh and easy*
	Young Vatted Spanish	
	Tempranillo La Mancha	*particularly fruity*
£4.00-4.50	Safeway Beaujolais	*flowery cherry fruit*
	◆ Cuvée Australe Syrah/	
	Grenache VdP d'Oc	*easy-drinking attractive fruit*

Cabernet Sauvignon and Sauvignon-based wines

£3.00-3.50	Safeway Young Vatted Bulgarian	
	Cabernet Sauvignon	*attractive easy-drinking*
£3.50-4.00	Kirkwood Moldovan Cabernet/	
	Merlot	*ripe and fruity*

Medium-bodied wines to serve on their own or with food

£3.00-3.50	Safeway Corbières	*easy-drinking fruit*
	Safeway Côtes du Rhône	
	◆ Safeway Sicilian Red	*easy-drinking*
	Don Darias Spanish Red	*oaky*
	Safeway Bulgarian Young	
	Vatted Merlot	
£3.50-4.00	◆ Château Montner Côtes du	
	Roussillon Villages	*fresh and juicy fruit with good length*
	● Safeway Chianti	*fresh and fruity*
	◆ Montepulciano d'Abruzzo	*good depth of fruit*
	◆ Safeway Casa di Giovanni	
	Sicilian Red	*oaky fruit*
	◆ Safeway Romanian Pinot Noir	
	Reserve Dealul	*rich vegetal fruit*
	Chilean Tocornal Malbec	*particularly fruity*

£4.00-4.50	◆ Zagara Nero d'Avola Vino da Tavola di Sicilia	*fresh cherry fruit with good depth*
£4.50-5.00	Domaine Vieux Manoir Maransan Côtes du Rhône	*good length of fruit*
	Cono Sur Chilean Pinot Noir Chimbarongo	*warm berry fruit*

Cabernet Sauvignon and Cabernet blends

£3.00-3.50	Safeway Young Vatted Cabernet Sauvignon Haskovo	
	Safeway Romanian Cabernet Sauvignon Reserve Dealul Mare	*easy fruity wine*
£3.50-4.00	Kirkwood Cabernet/Merlot	*ripe and fruity*
	◆ Safeway Chilean Cabernet Sauvignon Molina	*easy-drinking*
£4.00-4.50	Long Montain South African Cabernet Sauvignon	
£4.50-5.00	Safeway Claret Aged in Oak	*cedarwood and fruit*
	◆ Stony Brook Californian Cabernet Sauvignon	*spicy blackcurrant fruit*
	◆ Penfolds Rawson's Retreat Cabernet/Shiraz	*long blackcurrant fruit*

Heavier wines to serve with food

£3.00-3.50	Safeway Falua Ribatejo Portuguese Red	
£3.50-4.00	Safeway Bairrada Portuguese Red	
	◆ Safeway Casa di Giovanni Vino da Tavola di Sicilia	*full-flavoured plums with great depth*

£4.00-4.50	Safeway Oak Aged Spanish Valdepeñas Reserva	
£4.50-5.00	Tempranillo Oak Aged Rioja	*attractive oaky fruit*
	◆ Cosme Palacio y Hermanos Rioja	*particularly fruity*
	◆ Simonsvlei South African Shiraz Reserve Paarl	*long toasty coffee fruit*
	◆ Breakaway Australian Grenache/Shiraz	*good depth of blackberry and plum fruit*

Cabernet Sauvignon and Cabernet blends

£4.50-5.00	Jacob's Creek Australian Shiraz/ Cabernet	
	Settlers Creek Australian Shiraz/ Cabernet	*rich and chocolatey*

Good wines for parties

£3.00-3.50	◆ Safeway Sicilian Red	*excellent red berry fruit*
	◆ Vinenka Merlot/Gamza Reserve Suhindol	*easy-drinking red berry fruit*
£3.50-4.00	Brook Hollow Californian Red	*easy-drinking*

Splashing out

£5.00-5.50	◆ Penfolds Koonunga Hill Shiraz/ Cabernet Sauvignon	
£5.50-6.00	◆ Cosme Palacio y Hermanos Rioja	*particularly fruity*
	Wildflower Ridge Australian Shiraz	*luscious fruit*

£6.00-6.50 ◆ Villard Chilean Cabernet
Sauvignon   *long fruity wine*

Sainsbury

*T*here are now 360 Sainsbury stores and 11 Savacentres which also stock wine. These stores do cover the whole country but are mostly concentrated in the South. Wines are set out in two sections, red and white, and then by country and region. Some of these wines are available in this company's store in the Mammoth Shopping Centre in Calais.

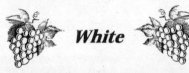

White

Fresh and light wines for easy drinking at any time

Under £3.00	Soave Superiore Sartori	*attractive honeyed fruit*	2
	Sainsbury's Chilean White		2
£3.00-3.50	Sainsbury's Trebbiano Garganega del Veneto	*fresh apples and pears*	2
◆	Portuguese Do Campo Branco	*very fruity*	2
	Hungarian Zenit Nagyrede Estate	*apple fresh*	1
£3.50-4.00	Sainsbury's VdP des Côtes de Gascogne Domaines Bordes		1
	Chenin Blanc VdP du Jardin de la France	*very fresh indeed*	1
	Sainsbury's Bordeaux Blanc	*easy spicy fruit*	2
	Bianco di Custoza	*fresh and fruity*	2
	Tuscan White Cecchi	*fresh and lightly oaked*	2
	Sainsbury's Pinot Grigio Atesino	*easy-drinking*	2

£4.00-4.50	Château l'Ortolan Entre-deux-Mers	*elegant gooseberry fruit*	2
	Sainsbury's Gaillac Blanc	*distinctive herby, spicy fruit*	1
	◆ Sainsbury's Grechetto dell'Umbria	*good depth of honeyed fruit*	2
£4.50-5.00	◆ Sainsbury's Cuvée Prestige Bordeaux Blanc	*elegantly fruity*	2

Sauvignon Blanc and Sauvignon-based wines

£3.00-3.50	Sainsbury's Ribatejo Sauvignon Blanc	*distinctive*	2
£3.50-4.00	Sainsbury's Touraine Sauvignon Blanc	*good gooseberry fruit*	1
	◆ Sainsbury's Sauvignon Blanc Ribatejo	*ripe herbaceous fruit*	2
	Gyongyos Estate Hungarian Sauvignon Blanc	*strong, minty and herbaceous*	1
£4.00-4.50	◆ Sauvignon Blanc Cave de la Cessane VdP d'Oc	*long, minty and herbaceous fruit*	1
	Sauvignon Blanc VdP du Jardin de la France	*easy minty fruit*	1
	◆ Chais Baumière Sauvignon Blanc VdP d'Oc		
£4.50-5.00	Sainsbury's Australian Semillon/Sauvignon	*easy tropical fruit*	2

Fuller-flavoured and fruity, but still relatively dry wines

£3.00-3.50	Sainsbury's Hungarian Irsai Oliver Balatonboglar	*distinctive grapey fruit*	2
	Sainsbury's California White	*particularly fruity*	2

£3.50-4.00	◆ St. Ursula Devils' Rock		
	Riesling	*fresh and grapefruity*	2
	Sainsbury's Australian White		2
£4.50-5.00	Marquès de Caceres Rioja		
	Blanco Crianza	*attractive lightly oaked fruit*	2
	Wynns Riesling Coonawarra	*particularly fruity*	2

Chardonnay and Chardonnay blends

Under £3.00	Rousse Bulgarian		
	Chardonnay	*fresh citrus fruit*	2
£3.50-4.00	Le Lizet VdP du Comte Tolosan		
	Colombard/Chardonnay	*minty citrus fruits*	2
	Sainsbury's Ribatejo		
	Portuguese Chardonnay	*distinctive*	2
	Sainsbury Khan Krum		
	Bulgarian Chardonnay	*oaky*	2
	Gyongyos Estate Hungarian		
	Chardonnay	*lightly tropical*	2
£4.00-4.50	◆ Chais Baumières Chardonnay		
	VdP d'Oc	*honeyed fruit with light oak*	2
	Chardonnay Cave de la		
	Cessane VdP d'Oc	*very fresh*	2
	Sainsbury's Chardonnay		
	delle Tre Venezie	*good fruit*	2
	Chardonnay Le Trulle Puglia	*honeyed apples and pears*	2
	Santara Spanish Chardonnay	*particularly fruity*	2
	Chapel Hill Estate Barrique		
	Aged Chardonnay	*attractive but very toasty*	2
	Sainsbury's Chilean		
	Chardonnay	*citrus fruits*	2

	◆ Barramundi Semillon/ Chardonnay South East Australia	*fresh and tropical with a touch of oak*	2
	Sainsbury's Tarrawingee Semillon/Chardonnay	*full and fruity*	2
£4.50-5.00	◆ James Herrick Chardonnay VdP d'Oc	*light tropical fruit*	2
	Lindemans Bin 65 Australian Chardonnay	*very oaky*	2
	◆ Saltram South Eastern Australian Chardonnay	*full ripe fruit with honey*	2
	◆ Penfolds Koonunga Hill Australian Chardonnay	*particularly fruity*	2

Medium dry, very fruity wines to serve at any time

£3.00-3.50	Sainsbury's Vinho Verde		4
£3.50-4.00	St Georg Morio-Muscat Pfalz		4
	St Ursula Devil's Rock Riesling	*lightly grapefruity*	4
	Sainsbury's Kabinett Rheinhessen Dalsheimer Burg Rodenstein		3

Sparkling wines for aperitifs and parties

£4.00-4.50	Sainsbury's Spanish Cava		2
£5.00-5.50	Sainsbury's French Chardonnay Brut		2
	Sainsbury's Australian Sparkling Wine	*apple fresh*	2
£5.50-6.00	◆ Sainsbury's Sparkling Saumur		1

| £6.50-7.00 | ◆ Spanish Vintage Cava Mont Marcal | | 2 |
| | Madeba Brut Robertson South African Sparkling Wine | | 1 |

Dessert wines

| £3.50-4.00 | Sainsbury's Muscat de St Jean de Minervois (half) | | 8 |
| | Sainsbury's Moscatel de Valencia | | 8 |

Good wines for parties

£3.00-3.50	Enclos des Lilas Blanc VdP de l'Aude	*easy-drinking pears*	2
	Sainsbury's VdP du Gers		2
	Sainsbury's Sicilian White	*simple and fruity*	2
	Sainsbury Valencia Oak Aged	*easy-drinking with light oak*	2

Splashing out

£5.00-5.50	◆ Sainsbury's White Burgundy Chardonnay	*good buttery fruit*	2
	Danie de Wet Grey Label South African Chardonnay	*very fruity*	2
£5.50-6.00	◆ Mme Gary's Block Chardonnay VdP d'Oc	*long toasty fruit*	2
	◆ Chardonnay Atesino Barrique Aged Vino da Tavola	*delicious oaky fruit*	2

Red

Light and fruity wines for easy drinking at any time

Under £3.00	Sainsbury's Valpolicella	*attractive easy-drinking cherry fruit*
£3.00-3.50	Sainsbury's VdP de l'Ardèche	*easy-drinking fruit*
◆	Costières de Nîmes Les Garrigues	*sweet bramble fruit*
	Sainsbury's VdP des Bouches du Rhône	*easy-drinking*
	Bulgarian Merlot Iambol Region	*plenty of soft fruit*
	Sainsbury's Do Campo Rosado	*easy sweet fruit*
£3.50-4.00	Domaine de Pujol Minervois Cave de la Cessanne	*flowery fruit*
◆	Merlot Atesino	*long fruity finish*
	Sangiovese di Toscana	*simple flowery fruit*
	River Route Romanian Pinot Noir	*attractive berry fruit*
£4.00-4.50	VdP de la Cité de Carcassonne Merlot	*ripe blackcurrant fruit*
	Beaujolais Village Les Roches Grillées	*good fruit*
	Solana Spanish Cencibel Valdepeñas	*fresh and fruity*

Cabernet Sauvignon and Cabernet blends

£3.00-3.50	Sainsbury's VdP d'Oc Cabernet/ Syrah	*light but attractive fruit*
£4.00-4.50 ◆	Sainsbury's Navarra Rosado Cabernet Sauvignon	*good depth of berry fruit*
	Sainsbury's South African Cabernet/Merlot	*good long fruit*

Medium-bodied wines to serve on their own or with food

£3.00-3.50	◆ Valpolicella Classico Sartori	*attractive mature fruit*
	Sainsbury Navarra	*simple easy-drinking wine*
	Sainsbury's Romanian Pinot Noir/Merlot Dealul Mare	
£3.50-4.00	Sainsbury's Côtes du Rhône	*simple easy-drinking wine*
	Bifino Campo Marino	*attractive toffee fruit*
	◆ Sainsbury's Mendosa Argentinian Sangiovese	*mixed berry fruits with blackcurrants and cedarwood*
£4.00-4.50	Sainsbury's Chilean Merlot San Fernando	
	Sainsburys's South African Pinotage	*good fruit*
£4.50-5.00	Domaine de Sours Rouge	*ripe vegetal fruit*
	James Herrick Cuvée Simone VdP d'Oc	*rich spicy vegetal fruit*

Cabernet Sauvignon and Cabernet blends

£3.50-4.00	Sainsbury's Claret	*easy-drinking*
	◆ Sainsbury's Cabernet Sauvignon VdP d'Oc	*attractive ripe fruit and liquorice*
	Morago Italian Cabernet - Sauvignon	*ripe warm fruit*
	Sainsbury's Reserve Bulgarian Cabernet Sauvignon Iambote Region	*appealingly long and fruity*
	Sainsbury's Chilean Cabernet Sauvignon	*good depth of fruit*
£4.00-4.50	◆ Chais Baumière Cabernet Sauvignon	*good blackcurrant fruit*

◆ Chais Baumières Syrah
VdP d'Oc

◆ Special Reserve Bulgarian
Cabernet Sauvignon
Iambol Region   *long blackcurrant fruit*

Special Reserve Bulgarian
Cabernet Sauvignon
Suhindol Region   *mature fruit with*
                          attractively long finish

Sainsbury's Mendoza
Argentinian Cabernet
Sauvignon/Malbec   *very fruity*

Sainsbury's South African
Cabernet/Merlot Reserve
Selection   *good fruit with real depth*

◆ Santa Carolina Chilean
Cabernet Sauvignon
Reserva Maipo   *particularly fruity*

£4.50-5.00 Sainsbury's Cuvée Prestige
Claret   *fruity and well balanced*

◆ Cabernet Sauvignon Atesino
Barrique Aged   *good balance*
                          blackcurrant fruit
                          and oak

◆ Sainsbury's Australian
Cabernet Sauvignon   *long blackcurrant fruit*

Nottage Hill Australian
Cabernet/Shiraz   *juicy berry fruit*

Heavier wines to serve with food

Under £3.00   Sainsbury's Portuguese Red

117

BEST WINE BUYS

£3.00-3.50	Sainsbury's Do Campo Tinto	
	Portuguese Red	*fresh berry fruit with black treacle*
	Sainsbury's Spanish El Gran Conde Vino de Mesa Oak Aged	
£3.50-4.00	Rosso del Salento Puglia	*hot raisin fruit*
	Negroamaro del Salento Italian Red	*attractive ripe fruit*

Cabernet Sauvignon and Cabernet blends

£4.00-4.50	Santa Carolina Cabernet Sauvignon Special Reserve	
	Tarrawangee Cabernet/Shiraz	

Good wines for parties

£3.00-3.50	Sainsbury's VdP de l'Aude	*simple easy-drinking wine*
	Sainsbury's Merlot Corvina del Veneto	*simple fruity wine*
	Sainsbury Valencia Oak Aged	*attractive easy-drinking wine*
	Sainsbury's California Red	*easy-drinking fruit*
£3.50-4.00	Sainsbury's Chilean Cabernet/ Merlot	*easy-drinking*

Splashing out

£5.50-6.00	◆ Bellingham South African Cabernet Sauvignon	*long ripe fruit*
	Penfolds Koonunga Hill Shiraz/ Cabernet	*good fruit and tar*
£7.50-8.00	Marquès de Murrieta Rioja Reserva	*deep vegetal fruit*

Somerfield

*T*his company also owns Gateway, Food Giant and SoLo and their wines lists are based on the list given below. There are currently 420 Somerfield stores and 250 Gateway stores giving national coverage of the UK.

The wines, which are arranged on the shelves by country and by region, are chosen for innovative quality and value for money. These stores do not have the space of some of the other supermarkets and every wine on the shelf has to justify its position.

White

Fresh and light wines for easy drinking at any time

£3.00-3.50			
◆	Somerfield VdP des Côtes de Gascogne Grassa	*fresh citrus fruits*	2
	Somerfield VdP des Coteaux de l'Ardèche	*apple fresh*	1
●	Somerfield Soave Pasqua	*easy honeyed fruit*	2
	Bianco del Monferrato Italian White	*good fruit*	1
	Estorila Branco Portuguese White	*floral fruit with honey*	2
	Santara Blanco Conca de Barbera Spanish White	*attractively fresh and fruity*	2

£3.50-4.00	◆ Domaine de Bordeneuve		
	VdP des Côtes de Gascogne		
	Grassa	*fresh and fruity*	1
£4.00-4.50	Soave Classico Vigneti		
	Montegrande Pasqua	*particularly fruity*	2

Sauvignon Blanc and Sauvignon-based wines

	Gyongyos Estate Hungarian		
	Sauvignon Blanc	*minty herbaceous fruit*	1
	Somerfield Chilean Sauvignon		
	Blanc Canepa	*particularly fruity*	1
	Sebastiani Californian		
	Sauvignon Blanc		1
	◆ Bellingham South African		
	Sauvignon Blanc	*green herby gooseberries*	1
£4.50-5.00	◆ Somerfield Oak Aged Bordeaux		
	Blanc	*good balance of oak and fruit*	2

Fuller-flavoured and fruity, but still relatively dry wines

£3.00-3.50	Somerfield Argentine White	*easy-drinking aromatic fruit*	2
£3.50-4.00	Pinot Blanc Trocken Gallerei		
	Rheinpfalz St Ursula		2
£4.50-5.00	◆ Viognier Chais Cuzac	*spicy, peachy fruit with good length*	2

Chardonnay and Chardonnay blends

£3.00-3.50	◆ Gandia Spanish Chardonnay	*apples and pears with light oak*	2
	Somerfield Hungarian		
	Chardonnay	*freshly aromatic and herby*	2
	Kirkwood Moldovan		
	Chardonnay	*lightly oaky fruit*	2

£3.50-4.00	Gyongyos Estate Hungarian		
	Chardonnay	*good fruit*	2
	Kumala South African		
	Colombard/Chardonnay	*fresh with good fruit*	2
£4.00-4.50	Somerfield Chardonnay		
	VdP d'Oc	*honeyed fruit with a touch of oak*	2
	Somerfield South African		
	Chardonnay	*good fruit*	2
£4.50-5.00	◆ Redwood Californian		
	Chardonnay	*lemon buttery fruit with oak*	2
	◆ Berri Estates Unwooded		
	Australian Chardonnay	*rich and fruity*	2
	◆ Somerfield Australian		
	Chardonnay Penfolds		2
	◆ Penfold's Bin 21 Australian		
	Semillon/Chardonnay	*good tropical fruit*	2
	◆ Penfolds Koonunga Hill		
	Australian Chardonnay	*good depth fruit and oak*	2
	◆ Hardy's Nottage Hill Australian		
	Chardonnay	*easy-drinking tropical fruit with oak*	2

Medium dry, very fruity wines to serve at any time

Under £3.00	Bulgarian Country White		
	Welsch Riesling/Misket	*fresh and flowery*	3
£3.00-3.50	◆ Somerfield Niersteiner		
	Spiegelberg Kabinett	*fresh flowery fruit*	4
£3.50-4.00	Somerfield Rheinhessen		
	Spätlese		4

Sparkling wines for aperitifs and parties

£4.00-4.50	◆ Chardonnay Brut Caves des Moines		2
£5.00-5.50	Somerfield Asti Spumante Araldica	*good grapey fruit*	7
	Seppelt Great Western Australian Brut Reserve		2
£6.00-6.50	Asti Martini Italian Sparkling Wine		7
£7.00-7.50	◆ Crémant de Bourgogne Caves de Bailly	*good depth of creamy fruit*	2

Dessert wines

£3.00-3.50	Somerfield Moscatel de Valencia	*particularly fruity*	7
£4.00-4.50	Somerfield Rheinhessen Auslese	*honeyed raisins*	7

Good wines for parties

£3.00-3.50	VdP du Jardin de la France Chardonnay	*easy-drinking apples and pears*	2
	Isola del Solle Sardinian White	*attractive lemony fruit*	2
	Somerfield South African Dry White	*boiled sweets*	2
£3.50-4.00	Somerfield Pinot Grigio del Veneto Pasqua	*apple fresh*	2

Splashing out

£5.00-5.50	Church Hill Australian Chardonnay Mildara	*lightly oaky tropical fruit* 2
£7.00-7.50	◆ Somerfield Chablis	*good depth of full fruit* 1
	◆ Sancerre	*fresh but elegant gooseberry fruit* 1

Red

Light and fruity wines for easy drinking at any time

£3.00-3.50	Somerfield Côtes de Gascogne Rouge Yvon Mau	*good berry fruit*
	Syrah Rosé VdP d'Oc	
	Somerfield Corbières Rouge	*fresh cherries and plums*
	● Somerfield Bardolino Pasqua	*good cherry fruit*
	● Somerfield Valpolicella Pasqua	*fresh and full*
£3.50-4.00	Somerfield Côtes de Roussillon Jeanjean	
	Somerfield Sangiovese Italian Red	*attractive fruit*

Medium-bodied wines to serve on their own or with food

Under £3.00	Somerfield Argentinian Red	*simple easy-drinking wine*
£3.00-3.50	Somerfield Bergerac Rouge Yvon Mau	*leafy blackcurrants*
	Somerfield Côtes du Rhône	*easy-drinking raspberry fruit*

	Somerfield Montereale Sicilian Red	*easy-drinking*
	◆ Santara Tinto Conca de Barbera Spanish Red	*ripe blackcurrant and bramble fruit*
£3.50-4.00	◆ Somerfield Fitou	*ripe, spicy, fruity*
	Montepulciano d'Abruzzo	*full and fruity*
	◆ I Grilli di Villa Thalia Southern Italian Red	*full ripe fruit with a touch of raisins*
	Stambolovo Bulgarian Reserve Merlot	
	Somerfield Californian Dry Red Sebastiani	*sweet berry fruit*
£4.00-4.50	◆ Somerfield Buzet	*attractive soft fruit with good length*
	Berberana Tempranillo Rioja Dragon Label	*oaky vanilla with sweet ripe fruit*
	◆ Kumala South African Cinsault/ Pinotage Western Cape	*spicy red berry fruit*
£4.50-5.00	◆ Redwood Trail Californian Pinot Noir	*ripe vegetal fruit with good length*

Cabernet Sauvignon and Cabernet blends

£3.00-3.50	●◆ Somerfield Claret Eschenauer	*easy-drinking fruit with a touch of cedarwood*
	Cabernet Sauvignon VdP Val d'Orbieu	*particularly fruity*
£4.00-4.50	◆ Landema Falls South African Cabernet Sauvignon	*ripe blackberry fruit*
£4.50-5.00	◆ Somerfield Oak Aged Claret	*good depth of fruit with cedarwood*
	Montana New Zealand Cabernet Sauvignon	*good blackcurrant fruit*

Heavier wines to serve with food

Under £3.00	Castillo Imperial Tinto Vino de la Tierra Manchuela	*warm jammy fruit*
£3.50-4.00	Senorio de Val Valdepeñas Crianza Spanish Red	*distinctively oaky*
£4.00-4.50	Hardy's Stamp Collection Australian Red	*warm blackcurrant fruit*
£4.50-5.00	◆ Château de la Valoussiere Coteaux du Languedoc	*attractive ripe, chocolate fruit*
	Vacqueyras	*ripe spicy fruit*
	◆ Crozes Hermitage	*deep vegetal fruit with liquorice*

Cabernet Sauvignon and Cabernet blends

£4.00-4.50	◆ Somerfield Penfolds Australian Cabernet Sauvignon	*rich fruit with liquorice*
	◆ Somerfield Australian Shiraz	*particularly fruity*
	Jacob's Creek Australian Dry Red	
£4.50-5.00	Penfolds Rawsons Retreat Bin 35 Australian Shiraz/ Cabernet	*blackcurrant fruit*
	◆ Hardy's Nottage Hill Australian Cabernet Sauvignon	*juicy red berry fruit*

Good wines for parties

Under £3.00	Somefield Bulgarian Country Red	*simple easy-drinking fruit*
£3.00-3.50	Somerfield VdP de l'Ardèche	*good fruit*
	Somerfield South African Red	*raspberry and strawberry fruit*

Splashing out

£5.00-5.50	Santa Rita Chilean Cabernet Sauvignon Reserva
£5.50-6.00	Senorio de Agos Rioja Reserva
	Marquès del Puerto *mature ripe fruit*

Spar

*T*here are nearly 2000 Spar off-licence shops spread across Britain. Store managers and owners within this marketing group may choose to stock any or all of the wines recommended below.

White

£3.00-3.50	Spar VdP de l'Aude	*fresh simple wine*	2
	Spar VdP des Côtes de Gascogne La Gelise	*fresh lemony fruit*	2
	◆ La Mancha Spanish White	*good depth of fragrant fruit*	3
£3.50-4.00	Spar Chenin Blanc DVP du Jardin de la France	*very fresh*	2
	Spar Muscadet de Sèvre-et-Maine	*apples and honey*	1
£4.00-4.50	Côtes de St Mont Tuilieres du Bosc		2
	◆ Paarl Heights Colombard	*fresh and fruity*	2
£4.50-5.00	◆ Torres Vina Sol	*fresh and fruity*	2

Sauvignon Blanc and Sauvignon blends

| £4.50-5.00 | ◆ Sable View South African Sauvignon Blanc | *minty gooseberries* | 1 |

Fuller-flavoured and fruity, but still relatively dry wines

Chardonnay and Chardonnay blends

£3.50-4.00	● Spar Chardonnay VdP d'Oc Cuxac		2
	Bulgarian Chardonnay Khan Krum	*oaky*	1
£4.00-4.50	◆ Dunavar Prestige Hungarian Chardonnay	*good buttery fruit*	1
	Chilean Chardonnay	*lightly tropical citrus and spicy fruit*	2
	Hardy's Stamp Series Australian Semillon/ Chardonnay	*particularly fruity*	2
	◆ Lindemans Cawarra Colombard/Chardonnay	*lightly tropical with a good finish*	2
£4.50-5.00	◆ James Herrick Chardonnay VdP d'Oc	*full and fruity with oak*	2
	◆ Sable View South African Chardonnay	*fresh and fruity with a touch of oak*	2
	Jacob's Creek Australian Chardonnay		2
	◆ Nottage Hill Australian Chardonnay	*easy-drinking tropical fruit with oak*	2

Medium dry, very fruity wines to serve at any time

£3.00-3.50	◆ Niersteiner Gutes Domthal	*fresh and grapefruity*	4

SPAR

Sparkling wines for aperitifs and parties

£4.50-5.00	Great Western Brut Australian Sparkling Wine	2
£6.00-6.50	Orlando Carrington Brut Australian Sparkling Wine	2

Dessert wines

£3.00-3.50	◆ Muscat St Jean de Minervois (halves)	*grapes and dried fruits*	7

Good wines for parties

£3.00-3.50	Spar VdP du Gers	*fresh and lemony pears*	2

Splashing out

£8.00-8.50	◆ Chablis Chablisiènne	*good steely fruit*	1

Red

Light and fruity wines for easy drinking at any time

£3.00-3.50	● Spar Cabernet Sauvignon VdP de l'Aude	*warm blackcurrant fruit*
	◆ Montepulciano d'Abruzzo	*fresh and attractive with good length*
£3.50-4.00	Spar Merlot del Veneto	*easy-drinking fruit*

129

| | Spar Sicilian Vin de Table | *warm and ripe but fresh fruit* |

£3.50-4.00	Merlot VdP d'Oc Cuxac Domaine Rivage	*good depth of attractive fruit*
£4.00-4.50	Spar Côtes du Rhône	*attractive easy-drinking wine*
	Spar Chianti	*warm cherries and raisins*
	Jacob's Creek Australian Dry Red	

Cabernet Sauvignon and Cabernet blends

£3.00-3.50	Bulgarian Country Red Russe Cabernet/Cinsault	*easy-drinking blackberry fruit*
	● Bulgarian Korten Cabernet Sauvignon	*hot blackcurrant fruit*
£3.50-4.00 ●◆	Spar Claret	*good balance of wood, tannin and fruit*
£4.50-5.00	◆ Sable View South African Cabernet Sauvignon	*good depth of fruit*
	◆ Chilean Merlot	*ripe blackcurrants with great length*

£3.00-3.50	● Don Darias Vino da Mesa Spanish Red	*ripe vegetal fruit*
£4.00-4.50	Vina Albali Reserva Spanish Red	
	◆ Lindemans Cawarra Australian Shiraz/Cabernet	*full and ripe blackcurrant fruit*

	Hardy's Stamp Series Australian Shiraz/Cabernet	*warm blackcurrant fruit*
£4.50-5.00	◆ Chilean Cabernet Sauvignon	*good depth of blackcurrants and blackberries*
	Nottage Hill Australian Cabernet Sauvignon	*juicy berry fruit*

Good wines for parties

£3.00-3.50	Spar VdP de la Cité de Carcassonne	*simple cherry fruit*
	◆ Bulgarian Merlot/Gamay	*attractive easy-drinking fruit*

Splashing out

£5.00-5.50	◆ Torres Coronas Penedès Spanish Red

Tesco

*T*his chain now has over 530 stores which spread right across the country from Elgin in the north to Haverfordwest in the west and Lowestoft in the east. Many of the wines can also be found at Tesco Vin Plus in Cité Europe, Calais. The wines are arranged on the shelves by colour and then by country.

 White

Fresh and light wines for easy drinking at any time

£3.00-3.50	◆ Tesco Escoubes VdP des Côtes		
	de Gascogne	*particularly fruity*	2
	Tesco Blayais Blanc	*apple fresh*	1
	Tesco French Semillon		
	Bordeaux	*good fruit*	2
	◆ Tesco Soave	*attractive apple-fresh fruit*	2
	Tesco Bianco del Salento	*fresh and fruity*	2
	Santara Spanish Dry White	*easy-drinking*	1
	Tesco South African Dry White	*easy-drinking*	2
£3.50-4.00	● Tesco Muscadet	*simple apple-fresh wine*	1
	◆ Barbi Bianco di Custoza	*fresh and fruity*	1
	Tesco South African Cape Chenin	*pears and apples*	1

132

£4.00-4.50	◆ Domaine Lapiarre Côtes du Duras	*spicy citrus and gooseberries*	1
	◆ Tesco Domaine Saubagnere	*fresh spicy grapefruit*	2
	Tesco Verdicchio Classico	*honied fruit*	2
	Château Passavant Anjou Blanc	*distinctive*	3
£4.50-5.00	◆ Château de la Coline Bergerac Blanc	*fresh with herby fruit*	2

Sauvignon Blanc and Sauvignon-based wines

£3.00-3.50	Tesco Chilean White	*particularly fruity*	2
£3.50-4.00	◆ Tesco Sauvignon Blanc Bordeaux	*light gooseberries*	1
	Tesco Sauvignon Blanc del Veneto	*lightly herbaceous*	2
	● Tesco South African White	*pleasantly spicy fruit*	
£4.00-4.50	Tesco Swartland South African Sauvignon Blanc	*lightly herby fruit*	1
	Tesco Australian Semillon/ Sauvignon	*distinctive citrus fruits*	2
	◆ Oxford Landing Australian Sauvignon Blanc	*herbaceous gooseberry fruits*	2

Fuller-flavoured and fruity, but still relatively dry wines

£3.00-3.50	Tesco St Johanner Abtei Dry	*fresh and fruity with a touch of honey*	2
	Servus Austrian Dry White	*attractively fresh*	1
	Chapel Hill Hungarian Irsai Oliver	*distinctively aromatic*	2
	Tesco Cape South African Colombar		2
£3.50-4.00	Tesco Australian White	*easy citrus and tropical fruits*	2

£4.00-4.50	◆ Tesco White Rioja	*full and fruity with oak*	2
	South African Barrel-Fermented Chenin	*fresh but toasty, attractive*	2
● ◆	Tesco Australian Rhine Riesling	*flowery fruit*	2
£4.50-5.00	◆ Salice Salento Bianco	*distinctively attractive citrus fruits*	2

Chardonnay and Chardonnay blends

£3.00-3.50	◆ Reka Valley Hungarian Chardonnay	*fresh citrus fruits*	2
£3.50-4.00	Tesco Bulgarian Chardonnay Reserve	*spicy lemon fruit*	2
	Tesco Brazilian Chardonnay/Semillon	*light oak*	2
	Tesco South African Cape Colombar/Chardonnay	*fresh fruit with honey*	2
£4.00-4.50	◆ Robertson South African Chardonnay	*ripe but fresh easy-drinking fruit*	2
	◆ Barramundi Australian Semillon/Chardonnay	*fresh and tropical with a hint of oak*	2
	Old Triangle Australian Semillon/Chardonnay	*well balanced oak and tropical fruit*	2
£4.50-5.00	◆ Chardonnay Reserve Maurel Vedeau	*good long fruit*	2
	Le Trulle Chardonnay del Salento	*full and honeyed with a touch of oak*	2
	Caliterra Casablanca Chilean Chardonnay	*oaky*	2

◆ Hardy's Nottage Hill Australian
  Chardonnay   *easy-drinking tropical*
                                fruit with oak   2
◆ Penfolds Koonunga Hill
  Australian Chardonnay   *fresh tropical fruit with*
                                medium oak   2
  Lindemans Bin 65 Australian
  Chardonnay   *very oaky*   2

Medium dry, very fruity, wines to serve at any time

£3.00-3.50	Tesco Riesling Mosel	*fresh and fruity*	4
£3.50-4.00	Tesco St Johanner Abtei		
	Spätlese	*distinctive fresh grape-*	
		fruit and raisin fruit	5

Sparkling wines for aperitifs and parties

£4.00-4.50	Sparkling Soave Spumante	2
£5.00-5.50	Tesco Asti Italian Sparkling	
	Wine	7
	Tesco Australian Sparkling	
	Wine	1
	Tesco South African Sparkling	
	Sauvignon Blanc Bergkelder	1
£6.00-6.50	Italian Sparkling Chardonnay	
	Spumante	2
	Angas Brut Australian	
	Sparkling Rosé	1
£7.00-7.50	Tesco Crémant de Bourgogne	1
	Australian Sparkling Chardonnay	2

BEST WINE BUYS

Dessert wines

£3.50-4.00	◆ Tesco Moscatel de Valencia		8
£4.00-4.50	◆ Muscat Cuvée José Sala	*grapey fruit*	8
£5.00-5.50	◆ Domaine de la Jalousie Late Harvest Grassa		6

Good wines for parties

Under £3.00	Bear Ridge Bulgarian Dry White	*soft spicy citrus fruits*	3
£3.00-3.50	Bergerac Blanc	*soft and easy-drinking*	2
	◆ Tesco Sicilian White	*attractively fresh and full flavoured fruit*	1

Splashing out

| £6.00-6.50 | ◆ Rosemount Australian Chardonnay | *well rounded and elegant fruit* | 2 |

 Red

Light and fruity wines for easy drinking at any time

Under £3.00	◆ Romanian Cellars Pinot Noir/ Merlot	*good fruit*
£3.00-3.50	● Tesco VdP des Bouches du Rhône	*simple fruity wine*
	● Tesco Corbières	*pleasant fruit*

◆ Tesco Domaine de Beaufort
    Minervois — *good depth of red currant fruit*

    Tesco Anjou Rouge — *easy-drinking fruit*

● Tesco Valpolicella — *easy-drinking cherry fruit*

    Tesco Italian Merlot del Piave — *good depth of fruit*

    Tesco Hungarian Merlot — *easy-drinking fruit*

£3.50-4.00 ◆ Tesco Bardolino — *red berry fruit salad*

    Tesco Rosé de Umbria — *light and fruity with rose petals*

£4.00-4.50 Les Vieux Cépages Cinsault
    Rosé — *easy-drinking and fruity*

    Tesco Merlot del Trentino — *attractive summer berry fruit*

Medium-bodied wines to serve on their own or with food

£3.00-3.50 Les Vieux Cépages Grenache

    Tesco Corbières Les Producteurs Reunis

◆ Grand Carat VdP du Comte
    Tolosan — *rich raspberry and red berry fruit*

    Tesco Rosso del Salento — *lightly distinctive raisiny fruit*

£3.50-4.00 Les Vieux Cépages Carignan — *vegetal fruit*

    Marquis de Chive Spanish Red — *attractive light oak*

◆ Tesco Bairrada Portuguese
    Red — *rich and mature*

◆ Tesco Domaine de la Source
    Syrah VdP de l'Hérault — *particularly fruity*

£4.00-4.50 Saumur Rouge — *toasty bramble fruit*

	Le Trulle Primitivo del Salento	*warm and fruity*
	Tesco Stellenbosch South African Merlot	*easy-drinking fruit*
	Tesco Australian Mataro	*particularly fruity*
£4.50-5.00	Tesco Chianti Classico	*fresh and fruity with good depth*
	Villa Boscorotondo Italian Red	*fresh fruit with a good finish*
	Barramundi Australian Shiraz/ Merlot	*warm bramble fruit*

Cabernet Sauvignon and Cabernet blends

£3.00-3.50	Tesco VdP des Côtes de Gascogne Rouge	
	Tesco French Cabernet Sauvignon VdP de la Haute Vallée de l'Aude	*pleasant shortish fruit*
	● Tesco Claret	*easy-drinking fruit with a touch of cedarwood*
	● Tesco Bulgarian Cabernet Sauvignon	
£3.50-4.00	Tesco Italian Cabernet del Veneto	*pleasant soft fruit*
	◆ Tesco Bulgarian Cabernet Sauvignon Reserve	*ripe vegetal fruit*
	Tesco Brazilian Cabernet/ Merlot	
£4.00-4.50	◆ Château les Valentines Bergerac	
	◆ Tesco Chilean Cabernet Sauvignon	*attractive juicy fruit*
	◆ Tesco Paarl South African Cabernet Sauvignon	*easy-drinking red berry fruit*
£4.50-5.00	Nottage Hill Australian Cabernet/ Shiraz	*juicy berry fruit*

Heavier wines to serve with food

£3.00-3.50	Tesco Chilean Red	*particularly fruity*
£3.50-4.00	◆ Tesco Coteaux d'Aix en Provence	*warm and vegetal*
	Tesco Marquès de Chive Spanish Red	*distinctive mellow fruit*
	Borba Alentejo Portuguese Red	*good depth of bramble and plum fruit*
	◆ Tesco Bairrada Portuguese Red	*juicy ripe fruit with vegetal depths*
	● Tesco Australian Shiraz/ Cabernet	*good fruit*
£4.00-4.50	◆ Casal Giglio Italian Shiraz	*particularly fruity*
	Tesco Australian Shiraz	*good fruit*
£4.50-5.00	Lindemans Bin 50 Australian Shiraz	*good depth of ripe fruit*

Cabernet Sauvignon and Cabernet blends

£4.00-4.50	Barramundi Australian Shiraz/Merlot	*warm bramble fruit*
	Oak Village South African Vintage Reserve (C)	
£4.50-5.00	Tesco South African Shiraz/ Cabernet	
	Penfolds Bin 35 Rawsons Retreat Australian Cabernet Sauvignon	*attractive, easy-drinking long fruit*

Good wines for parties

Under £3.00 ● ◆	Tesco VdP de l'Aude	*easy-drinking red berry fruit*

	● Tesco Sicilian Red	*easy-drinking sweet ripe fruit*
£3.00-3.50	Tesco Grenache	*light easy-drinking*
	● Tesco South African Red	*easy-drinking fruit*

Splashing out

£5.50-6.00	◆ Villa Pigna Cabernasco Italian Red	*excellent depth of fruit with a deliciously long finish*
	Tesco Chianti Classico Riserva	*fresh and fruity with a long finish*
	◆ Thomas Mitchell Cabernet/ Shiraz/Cabernet Franc	*good blackcurrant fruit*
£9.00-9.50	◆ St Hallets Old Block Shiraz	*wonderful depth of delicious fruit*

Thresher

*B*oth the 80 strong Bottoms Up chain of wine shops and the 120 strong WineRack chain are part of the same group as Thresher wine shops and there are 830 of these. Between them these stores cover the whole country.

All three chains have many wines in common. However, you may find some wines in Bottoms Up and WineRack which are not stocked in Thresher. If you cannot find one of the wines listed below in your local Thresher ask the staff to direct you to the nearest WineRack or Bottoms Up.

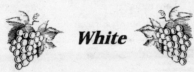

White

Fresh and light wines for easy drinking at any time

£3.00-3.50	◆ VdP du Gers Au Loubet	*fresh and fruity*	2
	Newlands Italian Vino da Tavola	*honeyed fruit*	2
£3.50-4.00	Le Cordon VdP d'Oc	*easy-drinking*	2
	Santara Conca de Berbera Spanish Dry White	*attractively fresh and fruity*	2
	Vega Camelia Rioja		1
	Stellenbosch South African Dry White	*fresh apples and pears*	1
	Paarl Heights South African White (Colombard)	*lightly spiced fruit*	2

£4.00-4.50	◆ Domaine du Tariquet VdP des		
	Côtes de Gascogne	*particularly fruity*	2
	KWV South African Chenin		
	Blanc	*good depth of fruit*	2

Sauvignon Blanc and Sauvignon-based wines

£3.50-4.00	Bordeaux Sauvignon	*excellent gooseberry*	
		fruit	1
	◆ Gyongyos Hungarian		
	Sauvignon Blanc	*gooseberry fruit*	1
	Las Colinas Chilean Semillon/		
	Sauvignon	*creamy grapefruit*	2
£4.00-.4.50	Kings Canyon Californian		
	Sauvignon Blanc	*particularly fruity*	1
£4.50-5.00	◆ Southlands Sauvignon		
	Blanc VdP d'Oc	*herby fruit*	1
	KWV South African		
	Sauvignon Blanc	*spicy gooseberry fruit*	1
	Winelands South African		
	Sauvignon Blanc	*attractive minty smoky*	
		fruit	1

Fuller-flavoured and fruity, but still relatively dry wines

£3.00-3.50	◆ Hungarian Country Wine		
	Muscat Riesling	*easy grapey fruity*	2
£3.50-4.00	Tollana Australian Dry		
	White	*spicy citrus fruits*	2
	◆ Penfolds Bin 202 Riesling	*distinctive citrus fruits*	
		and flowers	3
£4.00-4.50	◆ Las Colinas Semillon	*toasty citrus fruits*	2
£4.50-5.00	Sinnya South African White	*light citrus fruits*	3
	Tollana Coonawarra Australian		
	Riesling		3

Chardonnay and Chardonnay blends

£3.50-4.00	Bulgarian Reserve Chardonnay		
	Khan Krum	*oaky*	2
	Gyongyos Hungarian		
	Chardonnay	*lightly tropical*	2
	Tollana Australian Colombard/		
	Chardonnay	*particularly fruity*	2
£4.00-4.50	Soleil d'Or Chardonnay		
	VdP d'Oc		2
◆	Kirkwood Moldovan		
	Chardonnay	*easy-drinking oaky fruit*	2
£4.50-5.00 ◆	Southlands Chardonnay		
	VdP d'Oc	*full and fruity*	2
	Cool Ridge Barrel Aged		
	Hungarian Chardonnay	*well balanced oaky fruit*	2
	Cool Ridge Barrel Fermented		
	Hungarian Chardonnay	*easy-drinking well balanced fruit*	2
◆	Sinnya South African		
	Colombard/Chardonnay	*attractively fresh citrus fruits*	2
	Stellenvale South African		
	Chardonnay	*lightly oaky toasty fruit*	2
	Las Colinas Chilean		
	Chardonnay	*easy-drinking lightly tropical fruit*	2
◆	Santa Carolina Chilean		
	Chardonnay	*good fruit*	2
◆	Penfolds Koonunga Hill		
	Chardonnay	*particularly fruity*	2

BEST WINE BUYS

Medium dry, very fruity wines to serve at any time

£3.00-3.50	◆ Winelands South African		
	Medium Dry White	*easy-drinking flowery*	
		fruit	4
£3.50-4.00	● Bereich Bernkastel Gustav		
	Prinz		4

Sparkling wines for aperitifs and parties

£5.00-5.50	Castellblanch Spanish Extra Brut	1
£7.00-7.50	Lindauer New Zealand Brut	2
£7.50-8.00	◆ Seaview Australian Pinot/	
	Chardonnay	2

Dessert wine

£3.00-3.50	◆ Muscat VdP de la Collines de la		
	Maure (half)	*distinctively fruity*	7

Good wines for parties

£3.00-3.50	Domaine Bulgar Bulgarian		
	Chardonnay		2
	Butler's Blend Hungarian		
	Country Wine Pinot Gris/		
	Riesling	*flowery fruit*	3
£3.50-4.00	Winelands South African		
	Chenin Blanc	*easy-drinking*	
		grapefruit	2
	Las Colinas Chilean White	*spicy and lightly*	
		tropical	2

Splashing out

£5.50-6.00	◆ Ruppertsberger Linsenbusch Riesling Spätlese Rheinfpalz	attractively complex fruit	4
	◆ Villiera Gewürztraminer	lychees and spice	2
£8.00-8.50	◆ Church Road New Zealand Chardonnay	real depth of attractive fruit	2
£10.00-10.50	◆ Chablis Vieilles Vignes Defaix	distinctive fresh citrus fruits	2

Red

Light and fruity wines for easy drinking at any time

£3.00-3.50	● Le Coquelet VdP de l'Aude Red	attractively fruity
	VdP des Coteaux de Peyriac	easy-drinking
	Val du Torgan	excellent fruit
	◆ Santara Red Conca de Barbera	easy-drinking blackcurrant
	◆ J.P. Vinho Tinto de Mesa Portuguese Red	raspberry fruit
£3.50-4.00	Merlot Grave del Friuli La Rovere	attractive soft fruit
	◆ Valpolicella Merlot Tre Venezie	easy cherry fruit
£4.00-4.50	Winelands Cinsault/Tinta Barocca	attractive summer berry fruit

Medium-bodied wines to serve on their own or with food

£3.50-4.00	Figaro VdP l'Hérault	*good plum fruit*
	Faugère l'Estagnon	
	Fitou Special Reserve	*good depth of red berry fruit*
◆	Santa Carolina Merlot	*excellent depth of red berry fruit*
£4.00-4.50	Monte Ory Navarra Spanish Red	*particularly fruity*
	Quinta de Lamelas Douro Portuguese Red	*particularly fruity*
	Domaine les Colombies Corbières	
£4.50-5.00	Domaine Ste Eulalie Minervois	

Cabernet Sauvignon and Cabernet blends

£3.00-3.50	Domaine de Rivoyre Cabernet Sauvignon VdP d'Oc	
	Bulgarian Cabernet Sauvignon Plordiv Region	*good vegetal fruit with oak*
£3.50-4.00	Las Colinas Chilean Merlot/ Cabernet	*rich and plummy*
£4.00-4.50	Special Reserve Bulgarian Cabernet Sauvignon Iambol Region	*mature warm fruit*
£4.50-5.00	Bulgarian Controliran Cabernet Sauvignon Svischtov	*mature vegetal fruit with a touch of raisins*
	Winelands Cabernet Sauvignon/Cabernet Franc Stellenbosch	*blackcurrant fruit with plums*
◆	Sinnya South African Red	*good depth of plums and bramble fruit*
◆	Boschendal South African Red	*warm blackberry fruit*

Heavier wines to serve with food

£3.00-3.50	Copa Real	*ripe fruit*
£3.50-4.00	Dom Ferraz Bairrada	*good depth of mature ripe fruit*
£4.00-4.50	Twin Peaks Bulgarian Oak Aged Cabernet Sauvignon Rousse Region	*fresh with a touch of raisins*

Cabernet Sauvignon and Cabernet blends

£4.00-4.50	Tollana Australian Shiraz/ Cabernet	
£4.50-5.00	Fiuza Portuguese Cabernet Sauvignon Ribetejo	*hot ripe fruit*
	Winelands South African Premium Shiraz/Cabernet	*warm jammy fruit*

Good wines for parties

£3.00-3.50	Butlers Blend Country Wine Kekfrankos/Merlot Villany	*easy-drinking fruity wine*
£3.50-4.00	Côtes du Ventoux La Mission	*light and fruity*
	Moldova Kirkwood Cabernet/ Merlot	*easy-drinking ripe fruit*
	Paarl Heights South African Red	*attractive mixed berry*

Splashing out

£5.00-5.50	Château Guibon Bordeaux	*particularly fruity*
£5.50-6.00	◆ Château de Lastours Corbières	
	Campo Viejo Rioja Reserva	

Unwins

*T*here are 310 stores in this group based mainly in the South East with stores as far north as Leicester and as far west as Salisbury. Unwins are the largest independently owned off-licence group which has remained family-owned since 1843.

 White

Fresh and light wines for easy drinking at any time

£3.00-3.50	Ramada Portuguese White	*distinctive canned pears*	2
£3.50-4.00	● Muscadet de Sèvre-et-Maine		1
	◆ Côtes de Gascogne Domaine Lanine Yves Grassa	*fresh honeyed fruit*	1
	◆ Mauregard Petit Château Yvon Mau	*good depth of interesting fruit*	2
	Corbières Les Producteurs du Mont Tauch	*lemony honeyed fruit*	2
£4.50-5.00	Pinot Blanc Caves Vinicole de Turckheim	*fresh and fruity*	2
	Bianco di Custoza	*good fruit*	2
	Pinot Grigio del Veneto		2

Sauvignon Blanc and Sauvignon-based wines

£3.50-4.00	◆ Gyongyos Sauvignon Blanc	*gooseberry fruit*	1

| | Sauvignon Touraine | *gooseberry fruit* | 1 |
| ◆ | Sauvignon Yvon Mau | *elegant leafy fruit* | 1 |

Fuller-flavoured and fruity, but still relatively dry wines

£3.00-3.50	Tocai del Veneto Bartolomeo	*soft perfumed spicy fruit*	2
£4.00-450	◆ Austrian Pinot Blanc		
	Weinviertel Region	*full and fruity*	2
	Paarl Springs South African		
	Chenin Blanc	*fresh and fruity*	2
	Penfolds Stockman's Bridge		
	Australian White	*good tropical fruit*	2
	◆ Etchart Argentinian		
	Torrontes	*fresh aromatic and grapey*	2

Chardonnay and Chardonnay blends

£3.00-3.50	Bulgarian Chardonnay Russe		
	Region		2
£3.50-4.00	Hungarian Chardonnay		
	Mecsekalija Region		2
	◆ Domaine Collin Rosier		
	VdP d'Oc Chardonnay	*fresh and fruity with a touch of oak*	2
	Gyongyos Chardonnay HU	*lightly tropical*	2
£4.00-4.50	Hardy's Stamp Semillon/		
	Chardonnay	*particularly fruity*	2
£4.50-5.00	◆ James Herrick Chardonnay	*full and fruity with oak*	2
	◆ Sutter Home Californian		
	Chardonnay	*lightly tropical fruit and apples*	2
	◆ Nottage Hill Australian		
	Chardonnay	*easy-drinking tropical fruit with oak*	2

◆ Wakefield White Clare Crouchen/
Chardonnay   *tropical citrus fruits*   2

Medium dry, very fruity wines to serve at any time

£3.50-4.00   Lamberhurst Sovereign
English White   4
Mainzer Domherr Kabinett   4

Sparkling wines for aperitifs and parties

£6.00-6.50   Asti Martini Italian Sparkling
Wine   7
Carrington Extra Brut   2
£6.50-7.00   ◆ Cava Brut Methode
Traditionnelle Codorniu   *good earthy fruit*   2
Clairette de Die   *grapefruit and grapes* 2
Lindauer New Zealand Brut   2
£8.00-8.50   ◆ Vouvray Tete de Cuvée Brut   *lemon fresh and*
honcycd fruit   2

◆ Seaview Australian Pinot/
Chardonnay   2

Dessert wines

£4.50-5.00   Rivesaltes Vintage Vin Doux
Naturel   *rich dried fruits with*
damsons   8

Good wine for parties

Under £3.00   Bulgarian Country Wine Muskat
& Ugni Blanc   *easy-drinking*   3

Splashing out

£5.50-6.00	◆ Domaine de Tariquet VdP de Côtes des Gascogne Cuvée Bois	*oaky*	2
	◆ Penfolds Koonunga Hill Chardonnay		2
£9.50-10.00	◆ St Huberts Yarra Valley Australian Chardonnay	*extremly elegant with a touch of oak*	2

Red

Light and fruity wines for easy drinking at any time

£3.50-4.00	● Côtes du Roussillon	*good fruit*
	VdP des Côtes de Gascogne Michel de l'Enclos	*easy-drinking fruit and fudge*
	Montepulciano d'Abruzzo	*attractively long fruit*
	Weinviertel Blauer Zweigelt	*easy-drinking raspberries and blackberries*
	Penfolds Stockmans Bridge Australian Red	*easy-drinking red berry fruit*
£4.00-4.50	Valpolicella Classico	
	◆ Concha y Toro Chilean Merlot	*good depth of ripe fruit*

Cabernet Sauvignon and Cabernet blends

Under £3.00	Bulgarian Country Wine Cabernet Sauvignon/Merlot Pavlikeni	*easy-drinking fruit*
£3.00-3.50	Domaine St Denis VdP d'Oc Cabernet Sauvignon	*easy-drinking*

Medium-bodied wines to serve on their own or with food

£3.50-4.00	◆ Minervois	*fresh black cherries*
	◆ Fitou Producteurs de Mont	
	Tauch	*long warm fruit*
● ◆ Costières de Nîme Les Caves		
	des Apotres	*attractive ripe fruit with a touch of toffee*
£4.00-4.50	Chianti Villa Selva	*attractive fruit*
	Terras de Xisto Alentejo	
	Portuguese Red	*lush loganberries*
	◆ Borba Alentejo Portuguese	
	Red	*red berries and fudge*
£4.50-5.00	Cabardes Domaines de	
	Caunettes Hautes	*warm raspberries and plums*

Cabernet Sauvignon and Cabernet blends

£3.50-4.00	● Bordeaux Claret Yvon Mau	
	Hungarian Cabernet Sauvignon	
	Szekszard Region	
£4.00-4.50	Bulgarian Cabernet Sauvignon	
	Reserve Russe Region	
£4.50-5.00	◆ Mauregard Petit Château	
	Yvon Mau	*well balanced fruit and tannin*
	South African Cabernet	
	Sauvignon KWV	
	Sutter Home Californian	
	Cabernet Sauvignon	*good fruit*

Heavier wines to serve with food

£3.50-4.00	Pedras do Monte Portuguese Red	*vegetal fruit with liquorice*
£4.50-5.00	Dão Reserva Portuguese Red	*full fruit with old oak*

Cabernet Sauvignon and Cabernet blends

£4.00-4.50	◆ Hardy's Stamp Australian Shiraz/Cabernet	*easy-drinking*
	Jacob's Creek Australian Shiraz/Cabernet	
	Cahors Les Côtes d'Olt	*liquorice and eucalyptus*
£4.50-5.00	Madiran Les Vignerons de Buxet	*vegetal with strong tannins*
	Tollana Australian Shiraz Cabernet	*particularly fruity*
	Undurraga Chilean Cabernet Sauvignon	

Good wines for parties

£3.00-3.50	Merlot del Veneto	*easy-drinking*
	◆ Alto Mesa Portuguese Red	*fresh plums and cinnamon*
	Bulgarian Haskovo Merlot	

Splashing out

£5.50-6.00	◆ Fitou Château de Segure	*excellent depth of fruit*
£6.00-6.50	Wakefield Cabernet Sauvignon	*good fruit*

The Victoria Wine Company

*T*wo years ago this chain of high street off-licence shops bought the Augustus Barnett chain and the two were merged. Since then they have also taken over Thomas Peatling stores.

The Victoria Wine Company now trades as Victoria Wine Cellars (60 shops), Victoria Wine Shops (826 shops) and Neighbourhood Drinks Stores (483 shops), and Haddows in Scotland (182 stores).

All the wines listed below can be ordered by the single bottle from any shop if they are not in stock. The wines are arranged on the shelves by red and white and then by country.

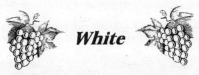

White

Fresh and light wines for easy drinking at any time

£3.00-3.50	● Victoria Wine French Dry		
	White VdP d'Oc		2
	Le Midi Blanc VdP de l'Aude	*honey fresh fruit*	2
	Castillo de Liria		2
	Hungarian Pinot Blanc		
	Nagyrede	*pleasantly honeyed*	2

154

£3.50-4.00	◆ Lurton Argentinian Chenin Blanc	*very attractive fresh spicy fruit with honey*	2
	Muscadet de Sèvre-et-Maine	*fresh and fruity*	1
£4.00-4.50	◆ Bois de Lamothe Côtes de Duras	*attractive lightly herby/ fruity*	1

Sauvignon Blanc and Sauvignon-based wines

£3.50-4.00	Bordeaux Sauvignon Calvet	*full herby fruit*	1
£4.00-4.50	◆ Sauvignon de Touraine, Hardy's	*fresh and elegant gooseberry fruit*	1
	La Serre Sauvignon Blanc VdP d'Oc		1
	Château la Tuque Bordeaux		1
£4.50-5.00	Philippe de Baudin Sauvignon Blanc VdP d'Oc	*ripe leafy gooseberries*	1
	KWV South African Sauvignon Blanc	*minty gooseberries*	1
	◆ White Ridge South African Sauvignon Blanc		1
	California Sauvignon Blanc Mohr-Fry Ranch	*very fresh minty gooseberries*	1
	◆ Casablanca Sauvignon Blanc	*herby gooseberries*	2

Fuller-flavoured and fruity, but still relatively dry wines

| £3.00-3.50 | Jose Niera Portuguese White | *oaky* | 2 |
| | Chapel Hill Hungarian Irsai Oliver | *distinctive aromatic fruit with grapes* | 2 |

£4.00-4.50	Big Frank's White VdP d'Oc	*good fruit*	2
	Long Mountain Chenin Blanc	*very fresh grapefruits*	1
◆	Cono Sur Chilean Gewürztraminer	*fresh flowery lychees*	2
	Nottage Hill Australian Rhine Riesling	*fresh tropical fruit*	3

Chardonnay and Chardonnay blends

£3.00-3.50	Landema Falls Colombard/ Chardonnay		2
£3.50-4.00	Chardonnay Vin de Pays du Jardin de la France	*fresh boiled sweets*	2
◆	Bright Bros Fernao Pires Portuguese Chardonnay	*fruity*	2
◆	Kirkwood Moldovan Chardonnay	*easy-drinking oaky fruit*	2
◆	Altura Chilean Chardonnay	*buttery apples and pears*	2
£4.00-4.50	Santara Spanish Chardonnay	*particularly fruity*	2
	Long Mountain South African Chardonnay	*lightly tropical with oak*	2
	Jacob's Creek Australian Semillon/Chardonnay		2
£4.50-5.00 ◆	La Langue Oaked Chardonnay Domaine Ste Madelaine VdP d'Oc	*fresh buttery fruit*	2
◆	Carmen Chilean Chardonnay	*easy-drinking, lush, fruity, lightly oaked*	2
◆	Hardy's Nottage Hill Australian Chardonnay	*easy-drinking tropical fruit with oak*	2
◆	Cooks Gisborne Hawkes Bay New Zealand Chardonnay	*full tropical fruit*	2

Medium dry, very fruity wines to serve at any time

£3.00-3.50	Russe Country Wine Muskat & Ugni Blanc	4
	Clearsprings South African Cape White	4
£3.50-4.00	Kabinett Bornheimer Adelberg	3

Sparkling wines for aperitifs and parties

£5.00-5.50	Victoria Wine Spanish Cava Brut	2
£6.00-6.50	Codorniu Première Cuvée Brut Spanish Cava	2
	Angas Brut Yalumba Australian Rosé	2
£6.50-7.00	Martini Italian Brut	2
	Asti Martini Italian Sparkling Wine	7
£7.00-7.50	◆ Graham Beck South African Brut	2

Good wines for parties

£3.00-3.50	Chapel Hill Hungarian Rhine Riesling	*easy, full and fruity*	3
£3.50-4.00	◆ Soave Pasqua	*attractive apple fresh fruit*	1

Splashing out

£5.00-5.50	Montana New Zealand Chardonnay Marlborough	*elegantly tropical fruit*	2
£5.50-6.00	Caliterra Casablanca Chardonnay	*tropical citrus fruits*	2
	◆ Yellowood Sauvignon Blanc	*elegant fruit*	1

La Langue Chardonnay/
Voignier VdP d'Oc Delta
Domaines   *spicy apple fruit*   2

 ## *Red*

Light and fruity wines for easy drinking at any time

£3.00-3.50	● Victoria Wine VdP d'Oc	*simple easy-drinking wine*
	Le Midi Rouge VdP de l'Aude	*good fruit*
	Costières de Nîmes	*good depth lightly vegetal fruit*
	Ashgrove South African Ruby Cabernet/Cinsault	*simple fruity*
£3.50-4.00	◆ Gamay de Touraine	*easy-drinking raspberry and cherry fruit*
	Abbaye St Hilaire Coteaux Varois	*easy-drinking fruit wine*
	Cortenova Italian Merlot Pasqua	*soft blackcurrant fruit*
£4.00-4.50	Grenache/Syrah VdP d'Oc La Baume	*very fresh tannic raspberries*
	Château de Capitoul La Clape Coteaux du Languedoc	*attractive fruit with good depth*
	Bright Brothers Terras Durienses Portuguese Red	*easy-drinking fruit*
£4.50-5.00	L.A.Cetto Mexican Petite Sirah	*full easy-drinking fruit*

Cabernet Sauvignon and Cabernet blends

£3.50-4.00	Hungarian Cabernet Sauvignon Szekzard

Medium-bodied wines to serve on their own or with food

£3.00-3.50	J.P.Vinhos Portuguese Red	
£3.50-4.00	Minervois Caves des Hautes	
	Coteaux	*fresh fruity cherries*
	◆ Sangiovese di Toscana Vino	
	da Tavola Cecchi	*attractively warm vegetal fruit*
£4.00-4.50	La Langie Merlot VdP d'Oc	
	Delta Domaines	*easy-drinking fruit with a touch of blackcurrant*
	◆ Big Frank's Minervois	*full ripe fruit with raisin finish*
	Concha y Toro Merlot/Malbec	*attractive blackcurrant fruit*
£4.50-5.00	Cono Sur Chilean Pinot Noir	*warm berry fruit*
	Carmen Chilean Merlot	*good depth of vegetal fruit*

Cabernet Sauvignon and Cabernet blends

£3.00-3.50	◆ Debut Cabernet Sauvignon	*mature woody fruit*
£3.50-4.00	Reserve Cabernet/Merlot	
	Suhindol	*mature fruit with black treacle*
	◆ Altura Chilean Cabernet	
	Sauvignon	*easy-drinking bramble raspberry fruit*
£4.00-4.50	● Victoria Wine Claret	
	◆ Long Mountain South African	
	Cabernet Sauvignon	*good fruit*
£4.50-5.00	Château Chantemerle Bordeaux	
	◆ Casablanca White Label	
	Cabernet Sauvignon	*fresh, fruity and long blackcurrants*

Heavier wines to serve with food

£3.00-3.50	Casa Barco Vino de Mesa	
	Oaked Spanish Red	*sweet mature fruit*
£3.50-4.00	Rama Corta Tempranillo	*robust wine with tarry*
	Cabernet Sauvignon La	*blackcurrants and*
	Mancha	*mocha*
£4.00-4.50	◆ El Liso Tempranillo La	*deep and warm vegetal*
	Mancha	*fruit*
	Special Reserve Cabernet	
	Sauvignon	*long elegant fruit*
£4.50-5.00	La Langue Domaine St Benoit	
	VdP d'Oc Rouge	*mature hot fruit*
	Chivite Reserva Navarra	

Cabernet Sauvignon and Cabernet blends

£4.00-4.50	Château Michelet Bordeaux	*tobacco and tar*
	◆ Hardy's Stamp Series Australian	
	Shiraz/Cabernet	

Good wines for parties

£3.00-3.50	● Castillo de Liria Valencia	
	◆ Ed's Red La Mancha	
	Tempranillo	*simple easy-drinking fruit*
	Hungarian Country Red	
	Kekfrankos Villany	*simple fruit*
£3.50-4.00	Lurton Bonarda Arg Red	*ripe brambles and plums*

Splashing out

£5.00-5.50	◆ Chivite Reserva Spanish Red	*well balanced fruit*
	◆ Rosemount Diamond Label	
	Shiraz/Cabernet	*mature summer berries*

Waitrose

*T*here are 116 stores scattered all over central and southern England from Sutton Coldfield and Peterborough in the north to Bath and Dorchester in the west. Greater London is particularly well covered to the west.

The wines are arranged on the shelves by style, though this method is currently under review. They are chosen with a view to presenting a wide assortment of interesting wines offering real value for money. As elsewhere space determines the number of wines on display.

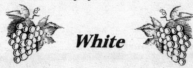

White

Fresh and light wines for easy drinking at any time

£3.00-3.50	Le Pujalet VdP du Gers	*flowery apples and pears*	1
£3.50-4.00	Domaine de Planterieu VdP des Côtes de Gascogne	*citrus fruits with a tropical note*	2
	◆ Pinot Grigio Vino da Tavola delle Tre Venezie	*attractively full and fruity*	2
	◆ Verdicchio dei Castelli Jesi	*lemony fruit with off dry finish*	2
	Deer Leap Hungarian Pinot Gris	*fresh and fruity*	2

	Culemborg Chenin Blanc Paarl		
	South Africa		1
£4.50-5.00	◆ Soave Classico Vigneto		
	Colombara	*fresh and fruit with good length*	2
	◆ Lugana Villa Flora Zenato	*particularly fruity*	2

Sauvignon Blanc and Sauvignon-based wines

£3.50-4.00	◆ Waitrose Bordeaux Sauvignon		
	Blanc	*attractive depth of elegantly minty fruit*	1
	◆ Domaine des Fontanelles		
	Sauvignon VdP d'Oc	*ripe fruit with a long finish*	1
	◆ Deer Leap Hungarian		
	Sauvignon Blanc	*minty herbaceous fruit with a hint of gooseberries*	1
£4.00-4.50	Touraine Sauvignon BRL		
	Hardy	*elegantly herbaceous gooseberry fruit*	1
	Les Voyageur Sauvignon		
	Bordeaux	*elegant well balanced fruit*	1
£4.50-5.00	Bellingham South African		
	Sauvignon Blanc	*very herbaceous minty style*	1

Fuller-flavoured and fruity, but still relatively dry wines

£3.00-3.50	Chapel Hill Hungarian Irsai		
	Oliver	*distinctively aromatic with grapes*	2
	South African Cape Dry		
	White	*particularly fruity*	2

£3.50-4.00	Deer Leap Hungarian		
	Gewürztraminer	*fresh and flowery*	2
◆	Waitrose Australian Riesling/		
	Gewürztraminer	*distinctively fruity*	2
£4.00-4.50	Penfolds Bin 202 Australian		
	Riesling	*distinctive citrus fruits and flowers*	2
	New Zealand Dry White		
	Gisborne	*particularly fruity*	2
£4.50-5.00 ◆	Laperouse Blanc VdP d'Oc	*lightly tropical fruit*	2
	Houghton Wild Flower Ridge		
	Australian Chenin Blanc		2

Chardonnay and Chardonnay blends

£3.00-3.50	VdP du Jardin de la France		
	Chardonnay	*easy almost herbaceous fruit*	2
	Clear Springs South African		
	Colombard/Chardonnay	*interesting, fruity*	2
£3.50-4.00	Terret/Chardonnay VdP d'Oc	*easy-drinking fruit*	2
	Lakeside Oak Hungarian		
	Chardonnay	*lightly oaky*	2
	Diamond Hills South African		
	Chenin Blanc/Chardonnay	*minty, lightly tropical*	2
	Santa Julia Argentinian		
	Chardonnay	*fresh apple fruit*	2
£4.00-4.50	Winter Hill Semillon/		
	Chardonnay VdP d'Oc	*attractive easy fruit*	2
	Hardy's Southern Creek Australian		
	Semillon/Chardonnay		3
£4.50-5.00	Chardonnay/Sauvignon Blanc		
	Domaine du Bousquet	*well rounded fruit with a touch of oak*	2
	Chardonnay (Matured in Oak) VdP d'Oc	*oaky with attractive balancing fruit*	2

Agramont Viura/Chardonnay	*long toasty finish*	2
◆ Springfield Estate South		
African Chardonnay	*well made, elegant Chardonnay*	2
Oxford Landing Chardonnay		
South East Australia	*easy-drinking and well balanced, oaky*	2

Medium dry, very fruity wines to serve at any time

£3.00-3.50	Tanners Brook English White Wine	*easy herby flowers*	2
	Waitrose Bereich Bernkastel		4
	Waitrose Piesporter Michelsberg		4

Sparkling wines for aperitifs and parties

£5.00-5.50	Le Baron de Beaumont Chardonnay Brut		2
	Santi Italian Chardonnay Brut		2
	◆ Waitrose Spanish Cava		2
	Seppelt Great Western Brut	*toasty*	2
	BB Club Hungarian Sparkling Chardonnay	*attractive and easy-drinking*	2
£6.00-6.50	◆ Waitrose Saumur Brut		1
	Angas Brut Australian Sparkling Rosé		2
£6.50-7.00	◆ Waitrose Blanquette de Limoux Brut	*good fruit and acidity*	1
	◆ Crémant de Bourgogne Blanc Lugny	*particularly fruity*	2
	◆ Crémant de Bourgogne Rosé Lugny	*good fruit*	2

Good wines for parties

| £3.00-3.50 | Winter Hill White VdP de l'Aude | *apple fresh* | 1 |

Splashing out

£5.00-5.50	Avontuur South African Chardonnay	*mature fruit*	2
£6.00-6.50	Villa Maria New Zealand Chardonnay	*well balanced fruit with light oak*	2
£6.50-7.00	Penfolds Organic Chardonnay/ Sauvignon Clare Valley	*well balanced oaky fruit*	2

 Red

Light and fruity wines for easy drinking at any time

£3.00-3.50	Winter Hill Red	*pleasant simple wine*
£3.50-4.00	◆ Domaine des Fontaines Merlot VdP d'Oc	*attractive earthy fruit*
	Sangiovese Vino da Tavola di Toscana	*easy-drinking red berry fruit*
£4.00-4.50	◆ Teroldego Rotaliano Ca' vit	*very attractive cherry fruit*
	◆ Canyon Springs Californian Pinot Noir Rosé	*very attractive and fruity*
£4.50-5.00	Waitrose Red Burgundy Boisset	*sweet berry fruit*

Cabernet Sauvignon and Cabernet blends

£3.00-3.50	Nagyrede Cabernet Sauvignon Rosé	*pretty fruity wine*
£3.50-4.00	Deer Leap Hungarian Cabernet Sauvignon/ Cabernet Franc	*fresh easy-drinking*
£4.50-5.00	◆ Avontuur South African Cabernet/Merlot Stellenbosch	

Medium-bodied wines to serve on their own or with food

£3.00-3.50	◆ Côtes du Roussillon	*long and fruity*
	Winter Hill VdP de l'Aude	*good depth of plums and red berries*
	◆ Bergerac Rouge	*easy-drinking fruit with a hint of cedarwood*
	Domaine de Rosé Syrah/ Merlot VdP d'Oc	*distinctive coffee flavours*
	Oriachovitza Barrel-Aged Merlot	*baked plums and blackcurrant fruit*
£3.50-4.00	Waitrose Côtes du Rhône	*flowery berry fruit*
	Montepulciano d'Abruzzo Umani Ronchi	*good depth of fruit*
	Waitrose Australian Malbec/ Ruby Cabernet	*attractive ripe fruit*
£4.00-4.50	◆ Ermitage du Pic St Loup Coteaux du Languedoc	*attractively long plummy fruit*
	◆ Fitou	*excellent depth of bramble earthy fruit*
	◆ Concha y Toro Merlot Rapel	*particularly fruity*
£4.50-5.00	Mâcon Supérieur Les Epillets Cave de Lugny	*ripe well balanced fruit*

Red Burgundy Pinot Noir
  Bourgogne Boisset   *light but good at the price*
◆ Cartlidge & Browne
  Californian Zinfandel   *toasty berry fruit with
     liquorice*

Cabernet Sauvignon and Cabernet blends

£3.00-3.50	Iambol Reserve Bulgarian	
	Cabernet Sauvignon	*ripe red berries*
£3.50-4.00	◆ Waitrose Good Ordinary	
	Claret	*excellent value for money claret*
	Foncalieu Cabernet Sauvignon	
	VdP de l'Aude	*fresh blackberry fruit*
	◆ Cono Sur Chilean Cabernet	
	Sauvignon	*intense blackcurrant jam*
	Santa Julia Argentinian Malbec/	
	Cabernet Sauvignon	
	Mendoza	*toasty depth of interesting fruit*
	◆ Diamond Hills South African	
	Pinotage/Cabernet	
	Sauvignon	*blackcurrant and bramble fruit with a long finish*
£4.00-4.50	◆ Du Toitskloof South African	
	Cabernet Sauvignon/	
	Shiraz	*attractive easy-drinking blackcurrants*
£4.50-5.00	Waitrose Special Reserve	
	Claret Côtes de Castillon	
	Graves Cordier	*woody blackcurrant fruit*

Heavier wines to serve with food

£3.50-4.00	Bulgarian Mavrud Reserve	
	Assengrad	*soft ripe vegetal fruit*
£4.00-4.50	Ribera del Duero Callejo	*distinctive vegetal fruit*
	Santa Carolina Chilean	
	Malbec	*leathery bramble and blackcurrant fruit*
£4.50-5.00	◆ Château Dt Auriol Corbières	*good depth of vegetal fruit with liquorice*

Cabernet Sauvignon and Cabernet blends

£3.50-4.00	Isla Negra Chilean Red	*strong blackcurrant fruit, hot and long*
£4.50-5.00	◆ Cosme Palacio Rioja	*rich vanilla fruit and a long finish*
	◆ Valdivieso Chilean Barrel-Fermented Cabernet/	
	Merlot	*wonderful depth of ripe fruit*
	Penfolds Rawson's Retreat	
	Bin 35 Australian	
	Cabernet Sauvignon	*attractive, easy-drinking long fruit*

Good wines for parties

Under £3.00	Ramada Tinto Portuguese	
	Red	*sweet ripe fruit*
£3.00-3.50	◆ Waitrose Merlot/Cabernet	
	Sauvignon VdP d'Oc	*easy-drinking blackcurrant and bramble fruit*
	Côtes du Ventoux	*easy-drinking and fruity*
	◆ South African Cape Dry Red	*fresh and easy-drinking*

Splashing out

£5.00-5.50	◆ Château Haut d'Allard Côtes de Bourg	*good vegetal fruit with cedarwood*
	Château La Vaviere Bordeaux Supérieur	*green pepper fruit, needs time*
	◆ Vale do Bomfim Reserve Douro	*ripe well balanced fruit*
	◆ Yaldara Whitmore Old Vineyard Australian Grenache	*particularly sweet ripe fruit*
£6.00-6.50	Cono Sur Chilean Pinot Noir Reserve	*good depth of vegetal red berry fruit*
	◆ Tatachilla Australian Cabernet Sauvignon McLaren Vale	*well balanced mature ripe fruit*
£6.50-7.00	◆ Hautes Côtes de Nuit Tete de Cuvée	*good depth of rich ripe fruit*

Wine Cellar

*T*here are around 19 Wine Cellar stores scattered across North Wales and Northern England and in the Greater London area. The 650 wines are set out by country and by wine growing regions.

Wine Cellar stores are part of the Greenall Cellars Group which also includes Berkeley Wines (stocking 450 of the total Wine Cellar range of wines), Cellar 5 (stocking 360), Greenall Food Stores (stocking 200) and Night Vision (stocking 200).

White

Fresh and light wines for easy drinking at any time

£3.50-4.00	Principato Valdadige Bianco	*very fresh fruit*	1
	Paarl Ridge Chenin Blanc	*herby citrus fruits*	1
£4.00-4.50	◆ Angelico Bordeaux Blanc	*full minty fruit*	1
	Viura Hermanos Lurton	*apple fresh*	2
	Torres Vina Sol		2

Sauvignon Blanc and Sauvignon-based wines

£3.50-4.00	◆ Andes Peaks Chilean Sauvignon Blanc	*easy-drinking minty fresh apples*	1
£4.00-4.50	Gemini Sauvignon Blanc Bordeaux	*elegant lightly herby fruit*	1
	Sauvignon d'Oc Lurton	*herbaceous fruit*	1

£4.50-5.00	◆ Sauvignon de Touraine Michel	
	Antier	*spicy catmint with ripe fruit on the finish* 1
	◆ Errazuriz Estate Chilean	
	Sauvignon Blanc	*good depth of minty apple fruit* 1

Fuller-flavoured and fruity, but still relatively dry wines

£3.50-4.00	Veijo Surco Argentinian	
	Torrontes/Chenin	*distinctive floral herby flavours* 2

Chardonnay and Chardonnay blends

£4.00-4.50	Chardonnay Barrique Aged	
	Balaton Winery	2
	◆ Andes Peaks Chilean	
	Chardonnay	*lush pineapple fruit* 2
	◆ Cordillera Estate Chilean	
	Chardonnay	*well balanced and fresh tropical fruit with oak* 2
	Bucklow Hill Semillon/	
	Chardonnay	2
£4.50-5.00	◆ James Herrick Chardonnay	
	VdP d'Oc	*full/fruity with oak* 2
	◆ Alasia Chardonnay Del	
	Piemonte	*fresh but buttery fruity* 2
	Santa Carolina Chilean	
	Chardonnay/Semillon	*ripe tropical fruits with a touch of toasty oak* 2
	◆ Glen Ellen California	
	Chardonnay	*attractive aromatic fruit with a touch of buttery oak* 2

BEST WINE BUYS

Medium dry, very fruity wines to serve at any time

£3.00-3.50	Bulgarian Muscat/Ugni Blanc Russe	*fruity*	4
£4.00-4.50	Riesling Mosel Saar Ruwer	*flowery grapefruit*	4

Sparkling wines for aperitifs and parties

£4.50-5.00	Seppelts Great Western Australian Brut		2
£5.50-6.00	Chardonnay Vin Mousseux		2
£6.00-6.50	Angas Australian Brut		1
£7.00-7.50	Cray, Crémant de Loire le Chapelle de Cray	*very dry fruit*	2
	Lindauer New Zealand Brut		1

Good wines for parties

£3.50-4.00	Bucklow Hill Australian Dry White	*tropical fruit*	2

Splashing out

£5.00-5.50	Decapole, Cave de Turckheim Alsace	*flowery, spicy fruit with a touch of honey*	2
£6.00-6.50	Bacchus Chapel Down Vineyards English Wine	*distinctive, searingly fresh and minty*	1
£9.50-10.00 ◆	Chablis Premier Cru Vaillons, Domaine Moreau	*excellent fresh lemons and apples with a touch of oak and a long fruity finish*	1

Red

Light and fruity wines for easy drinking at any time

£3.50-4.00	River Route Hungarian	
	Merlot	*light and fruity*
	◆ Montepulciano d'Abruzzo	
	Umani Ronchi	*very fresh and fruity*
	Haskovo Winery Bulgarian	
	Merlot	
	Canepa Chilean Merlot	*soft milky fruit*
	Paarl Ridge South African	
	Red	*cherry berry fruit*
£4.00-4.50	Breganze Rosso Cantine	
	Bartolemo	*easy-drinking milky fruit*
	Barossa Valley Australian	
	Grenache Peter Lehmann	*easy-drinking summer berries*
£4.00-4.50	Saumur Rouge Domaine des	
	Salaises	*easy-drinking ripe bramble fruit*
	Lurton Argentinian Malbec/	
	Tempranillo	*easy-drinking fruit*
	◆ Errazuriz Estate Chilean	
	Merlot	*attractive ripe berry fruit with toasty overtones*

Medium-bodied wines to serve on their own or with food

£3.50-4.00	Pedras do Monte Portuguese	
	Red	*very fresh*
	◆ Bucklow Hill Australian	
	Dry Red	*easy blackcurrant and red berry fruit*

173

£4.00-4.50	Syrah VdP d'Oc	*vegetal fruit with chocolate*
	Merlot VdP d'Oc Lurton	
£4.50-5.00	◆ Baso Garnacha Navarra	*summer berry fruits*
	Ruiteravlei South African Cinsault, Paarl	*fudge and fruit with a long hot finish*

Cabernet Sauvignon and Cabernet blends

£3.50-4.00	Hungarian Cabernet Sauvignon Villany Hills	
	Veijo Surco Argentinian Sangiovese/Cabernet	
£4.00-4.50	Palmeras Estate Chilean Cabernet Sauvignon	*soft ripe fruit with a long hot finish*
	Bucklow Hill Shiraz/Cabernet	*soft easy-drinking fruit*
£4.50-5.00	◆ Copertino Rosso Reserva	*fresh raisiny fruit*
	◆ Landscape South African Merlot/Cabernet	*long blackcurrant fruit*
	Canepa Chilean Cabernet Sauvignon	*attractive blackcurrant fruit with a little hot tar*
	◆ Domaine Apalta Villa Montes Chilean Cabernet Sauvignon	*well balanced attractive berry fruit with good attack*
	La Palma Vina la Rosa Chilean Reserve Cabernet Sauvignon	*attractive milky fruit with good acidity*

Heavier wines to serve with food

£4.00-4.50	Albor Cammpo Veijo Rioja	*easy-drinking chocolatey fruit*
£4.50-5.00	Campo Veijo Crianza Rioja	
	◆ Las Campanas Navarra	*mature vegetal fruit*

Good wines for parties

£3.50-4.00	Minervois Jeanjean	*attractive fresh and fruity*
	Argentinian Balbi Vineyard	
	Mendosa Rouge	*simple but pleasant*

Splashing out

£5.00-5.50	Ruiteravlei South African Cabernet Sauvignon, Paarl	*light blackcurrant fruit with good length*
£5.50-6.00	◆ Columbia Crest Columbia Valley Cabernet Sauvignon	*minty blackcurrant with good balancing acidity*
	◆ Château de Beaulieu Côtes de Marmandais	*attractive plummy fruit with good length*
£6.50-7.00	◆ Columbia Crest Columbia Valley Merlot	*good depth of ripe blackcurrant fruit*
	◆ Santa Isabel Estate, Vina Casablanca Chilean Cabernet Sauvignon	*deliciously ripe and well balanced blackcurrant fruit*

◆ Rosemount Estate
   Australian Merlot *long and attractive minty*
   blackcurrants

*T*his chain of high street off-licences is now part of the Thresher Group and many of the same wines are stocked in both stores, though WineRack does stock some wines which do not appear on the shelves at Thresher. However, because of the size of the overlap I have listed all my recommendations for both stores under Thresher on page 141.

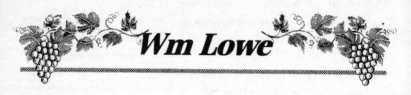

*T*his Scottish chain has been bought out by Tesco and all stores will become Tesco stores (see page 132).

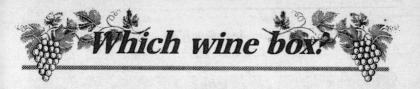

Which wine box?

*W*ine boxes are here to stay. They now account for around 7¹/₂% of the total wine market in the UK. This is equivalent to a huge three million plus cases, or 36 million bottles, of wine.

Contrary to the beliefs of some, wine boxes are not always the lowest common denominator. They follow the general taste – witness the trend towards varietal labelling of the contents – but many of them contain wine with which even the most discerning wine-drinker would be happy.

Wine boxes present wine in an easy-to-use container which will keep the wine fresh for at least two to three weeks, and they are no longer bought just for party use. Wine boxes are an attractive buy for anyone who likes to have a glass or two of wine on hand without having to finish a whole bottle. The wines are designed to be drunk and enjoyed at once. They are not wines which need time to mature.

Despite the fact that you are buying in larger quantities wine box wine is not very much cheaper than that in a bottle. This is because efficient packaging is expensive. However, the more you pay for your wine box the better the price comparison is likely to be. New Zealand Sauvignon Blanc, for example, can be bought for around £15.99 for a three-litre carton whereas the equivalent four bottles of most brands will cost rather more.

There are currently more than 100 different wine boxes on sale in the high street. During the research for this book I tasted about 80, rating them on a scale of one to ten. The results are set below along with a short tasting note for each box. Details of where to find the different boxes are also listed. All the wines are perfectly clean and acceptable, but those at the four/five level are not very interesting. More complex and fruity wines come in at six to seven plus.

Australia

White

Australian Dry White

Darlington Wines — *Plenty of easy-drinking tropical citrus fruits* — 8 points

Outlets: — Asda, Makro, Morrisons, Somerfield

Colombard/Chardonnay

McWilliams — *Attractive fruit* — 7 points

Outlets: — Morrisons, Somerfield, Waitrose

Semillon/Chardonnay

Barramundi — *Fresh and tropical*

Outlets: — Co-op

Stowells of Chelsea — *Attractive citrus fruits with easy oak* — 9 points

Outlets: — Safeway, Sainsbury, Somerfield, Tesco, Thresher, Unwins, Victoria Wine

Red

Australian Dry Red

Darlington Wines — *Massive red berry fruit, very attractive* — 9 points

Outlets: — Makro, Morrisons, Somerfield

Quagga — *Reasonable fruit* — 4 points

Outlets: — Safeway

Shiraz/Cabernet

McWilliams	*Good fruit*	7 points
Outlets:	Morrisons, Somerfield, Waitrose	
Stowells of Chelsea	*Attractive length of spicy plums with herbs*	9 points
Outlets:	Makro, Sainsbury, Somerfield, Tesco, Thresher, Victoria Wine	

Shiraz/Merlot

Barramundi	*Easy-drinking fruit*	7 points
Outlets:	Co-op, Safeway	

Bulgaria

Red

Cabernet Sauvignon

Co-op Own Label	*Quite good depth of red berry fruit*	7 points
Darlington Wines	*Mature fruit*	6 points
Outlets:	Asda, Morrisons	
Morrison Own Label	*Reasonable fruit*	6 points
Safeway Own Label	*Attractively light and fruity*	7 points
Sainsbury Own Label	*Distinctive style*	4 points
Stowells of Chelsea	*Distinctive aroma of green nuts*	4 points
Outlets:	Waitrose	
Tesco Own Label	*Pleasantly fruity*	7 points
Unwins Own Label	*Vegetal fruits*	5 points

Victoria Wine Own Label *Reasonable fruits*   5 points

Chile

White

Chilean White
Alto Plano   *Distinctive citrus fruits*   6 points
Outlets: Asda

Sauvignon Blanc
Stowells of Chelsea   *Very fresh ripe and herbaceous*
                                fruit   8 points
Outlets: Fullers, Morrisons, Victoria Wine,
                                Waitrose

Red

Cabernet/Merlot
Sainsbury Own Label   *Attractive easy drinking*   8 points

Chilean Red
Alto Plano   *Easy-drinking fruit*   6 points
Outlets: Asda

Merlot/Cabernet
Stowells of Chelsea   *Warm blackcurrants with*
                                liquorice   9 points
Outlets: Morrisons, Tesco, Victoria Wine,
                                Waitrose

France

White

Muscadet

Stowells of Chelsea	*Fresh apples*	5 points
Outlets:	Co-op, Leo's, Pioneer, Safeway	
Tesco Own Label	*Simple apple fresh with a touch of honey*	5 points
Unwins Own Label	*Honeyed mineral fruit*	4 points

VdP du Catalan

Co-op Own Label	*Very fresh*	4 points
Outlets:	Co-op, Leo's, Pioneer	

VdP des Côtes de Gascogne

Morrisons Own Label	*Particularly fruity*	7 points
Sainsbury Own Label	*Fresh and reasonably fruity*	6 points
Tesco (Escoubes) Own Label	*Attractive fresh lemony fruit*	7 points
Unwins Own Label	*Fresh and pleasantly fruity*	6 points

VdP des Côtes du Luberon

Safeway Own Label	*Simple easy-drinking wine*	5 points

VdP du Gers

Marks & Spencer Own Label	*Apple fresh*	5 points

VdP d'Oc Chardonnay

Sainsbury Own Label	*Very fresh*	4 points

Unwins Own Label	*Good honeyed pears and apples*	7 points

VdP du Tarn

Stowells of Chelsea Outlets:	*Attractive apples and honey* Asda, Budgen, Co-op, Fullers, Leo's, Londis, KwikSave, Somerfield, Thresher, Victoria Wine	7 points

Vin Blanc Sec

Waitrose Own Label	*Fresh but not very fruity*	4 points

Red

Claret

Co-op Own Label Outlets:	*Some soft fruit with low tannin* Co-op, Leo's	5 points

Safeway Own Label	*Attractively fruity with a hint of cedarwood*	8 points

Stowells of Chelsea Outlets:	*Well balanced cedarwood and fruit* Makro, Morrisons	8 points

Tesco Own Label	*Easy-drinking fruit with a touch of cedarwood*	6 points

Corbières

Sainsbury Own Label	*Good depth of fruit*	6 points

Tesco Own Label	*Pleasant fruit*	6 points

Côtes du Rhône
Somerfield (Villages)
Own Label   *Long easy-drinking raspberry fruit*   8 points

Tesco Own Label   *Straightforward wine*   4 points

Unwins Own Label   *Good length of plums and raspberry
                          fruit*   9 points

VdP de l'Ardèche
Sainsbury Own Label *Easy-drinking fruity*   6 points

VdP des Côtes du Luberon
Safeway Own Label   *Simple bramble fruit*   7 points

VdP d'Oc Cabernet Sauvignon
Sainsbury Own Label *Very fresh with some fruit*   5 points

Unwins Own Label   *Reasonable fruit*   6 points

VdP du Gard
Stowells of Chelsea *Easy-drinking warm and fruity*   5 points
Outlets: Asda, Budgens, Co-op, Fullers, Leo's,
                         Londis, Makro, Safeway,
                         Somerfield, Thresher, Victoria Wine

Hungary

White

Chardonnay
Safeway Own Label   *Lightly honeyed fruit*   5 points

Country White
Stowells of Chelsea   *Easy-drinking zingy spicy fruit*   7 points
Outlets: Co-op, Sainsbury, Wine Cellar

Italy

White

Chardonnay
Marks & Spencer Own   *Fresh pears*
6 points
    Label (Delle Tre Venizie)

Stowells of Chelsea   *Fresh pears and honey*   6 points
Outlets: Budgens, Leo's, Morrison, Pioneer, Tesco, Waitrose

Soave
Darlington Wines   *Extremely fresh with really good fruit*   8 points
Outlets: Asda, Co-op

Marks & Spencer Own Label   *Apples, pears and a little honey*   6 points

Tesco Own Label   *Simple clean wine*   4 points

Waitrose Own Label   *Fresh with a little fruit*   5 points

Red

Montepulciano d'Abruzzo

Marks & Spencer Own Label	*Really attractive berry fruit*	8 points

Montepulciano del Molise

Stowells of Chelsea	*Warm cherry fruit, easy drinking*	8 points
Outlets:	Sainsbury	

Valpolicella

Darlington Wines	*Good cherry fruit*	7 points
Outlets:	Makro	
Waitrose	*Very fresh with some fruit*	5 points

New Zealand

White

Sauvignon Blanc

Stowells of Chelsea	*Lemon fresh and leafy, very attractive*	9 points
Outlets:	Safeway, Tesco, Thresher	

South Africa

White

Chenin Blanc

Darlington Wines	*Sharp apples*	4 points
Outlet:	Leo's, Waitrose	

Stowells of Chelsea   *Pleasant easy-drinking wine*   5 points
Outlets: Budgens, Davisons, Makro, Morrisons,
                                          Tesco, Thresher, Victoria Wine

South African White
Clearsprings Cape Dry   *Fresh and fruity*   6 points
Outlet: KwikSave, Somerfield, Tesco

Marks & Spencer   *Full spicy fruit*   7 points
Own Label

Namaqua   *Easy fruit*   6 points
Outlets: Co-op, Leo's, Pioneer, Safeway

Tesco Own Label   *Soft and lightly spicy*   4 points

Red

Cinsault/Ruby Cabernet
Darlington Wines   *Good red berry fruit, very dry*   7 points
Outlet: Co-op

Pinotage
Stowells of Chelsea   *Attractively fruity*   6 points
Outlets: Co-op, Davison, Tesco, Thresher

South African Red
Clearsprings Cape   *Pleasant fruit*   5 points
Outlets: KwikSave, Somerfield, Tesco

Spain

Red

Tempranillo

Marks & Spencer　　　　*Liquorice hot*　　　　　　　　5 points
　Own Label

Stowells of Chelsea　　　*Good easy-drinking fruit*　　　8 points
Outlets:　　　　　　　　　　Budgens, Co-op, Fullers, KwikSave,
　　　　　　　　　　　　　　Leo's, Makro, Morrisons, Pioneer,
　　　　　　　　　　　　　　Safeway, Sainsbury, Somerfield,
　　　　　　　　　　　　　　Tesco, Unwins, Waitrose

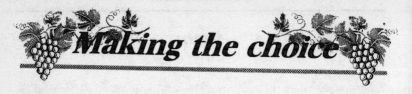

Making the choice

*H*ow much does it cost? What does it taste like? What is the occasion? These are the three questions which are likely to be going though your mind when you buy a bottle of wine.

You can see the price and you know the occasion but deciding on what the wine will taste like is a little more difficult. However, the front and back labels on the bottle can give you some information and shelf descriptions and taste guides add some more.

You may have a preference for particular grape varieties and an increasing number of wine-producing regions are adding this information to the label. Of course, you still need to know that Bordeaux reds will be a mixture of Cabernet Sauvignon, Merlot and Cabernet Franc and that white Sancerre is made from Sauvignon Blanc.

Assessing prices

Perhaps the most important criterion in wine buying today is the price tag and the vast majority of wine sold in the high street costs between £2.50 and £3.50. Not very many of us are prepared to pay more than £4.00.

Wine buyers have worked hard to keep the price of popular wines below the £3.00 threshold but there is only so far that they can go before the strain begins to show. Wines at this level have been reasonably well made but they tend to be very uninteresting. Increasingly the quality is suffering as well.

At prices under £3.00 very little of the money you pay goes to the grower or wine producer. Most of it goes to the tax man and the middleman. So, the amount actually spent on the raw material (the wine) is minimal. A relatively small increase in price can double the money going to the producer and so result in a big leap in the quality of the wine in your glass.

Buying wine solely on price is a mistake. If you possibly can pay 50p or even £1 more, you will experience the difference in the smell and the taste and hence in your enjoyment of the wine.

However, if you have time and transport you can often cut your wine costs by shopping around. All the supermarkets and many of the high street off-licence chains run regular monthly promotions with special cut prices, multiple sales offers and other promotions. Shopping in bulk by the case (twelve bottles) also attracts discounts of 5% or even 10%. Check with your local stores for details.

Reading labels

The front labels of bottles rarely spell out the character of the wine in so many words but they can give you enough information to form some idea of the taste and style. For example, wines from European countries will tell you which wine-producing region the wine is from and at what level it is at on the Appellation Contrôlée scales. If you see that a wine is from Beaujolais, experience of other wines from this area will tell you that the wine will probably be light and fruity.

Other wines, such as wines from Chile and Australia, tell you which grape variety has been used to make the wine. Chardonnay and Cabernet Sauvignon are popular grape varieties here and you may have an idea of what they are likely to taste like.

Vintage dates can tell you how mature the wine will be and whether or not it was made in a particularly good year. Some wines will also tell you how the wine has been matured. For example, barrel-aged and oak-aged wine will give you a further clue to the taste of the wine.

Origins

All labels tell you which country the wine comes from and may tell you which region within that country. Thus, if you have drunk an Italian Valpolicella with your lasagne or a Listel Gris de Gris with your salade nicoise and found that the combinations worked, you should easily find them again.

For countries which have an appellation or classification system the label will tell you whether the contents of the bottle are of the basic easy-drinking, party wine variety or are 'fine' wines from prestigious regions or estates. The price will also probably tell you this too!

In most of the countries of western Europe the cheapest level of wine is simply labelled table wine (Vin de Table in France). This everyday wine comes from anywhere in the country named. Next in line are the easy-drinking country wines (Vin de Pays in France). Above these are the Appellation Contrôlée or quality wines from smaller designated wine-producing areas.

On the next pages there are some typical wine labels from a variety of countries.

France

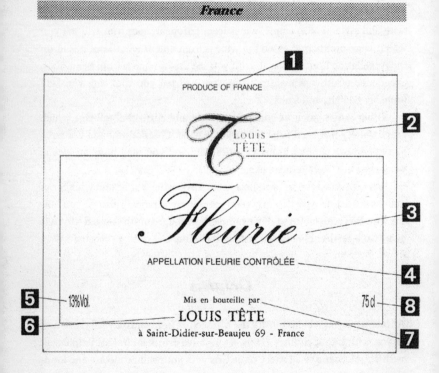

The label from the Beaujolais region does not carry the vintage as this was given on a small label just under the neck of the bottle. The following information is given:

190

◆   1. A declaration of the country of origin
◆   2. The name of the producer or bottler
◆   3. The wine region
◆   4. The AC declaration of origin which shows that the wine comes from
     the designated Fleurie region. Some wines from Bordeaux, Burgundy,
     Alsace and Champagne carry further classifications of the villages or
     estates from which they come
◆   5. The alcohol content of the wine
◆   6. The name and address of the producer or bottler
◆   7. The declaration of where the wine was bottled, in this case at the
     premises of Louis Tête. The chances are that Louis Tête is a négociant
     and bottler, buying wine from other producers. Compare the statement
     here to the '*Mis en bouteille au château or au domaine*' which you may
     find on other bottles. The latter statement means that the wine was
     bottled on the estate where it was produced
◆   8. The contents of the bottle

Other phrases which you might see on a French label include:
◆   Blanc de Blanc – wine made from white grapes only
◆   Blanc de Noir – white wine made from black grapes
◆   Supérieur – higher alcohol content to the regular wine
◆   Récolte du domaine – the produce of a single estate

You may sometimes see other phrases on the label such as '*grand vin*',
'*sélection spéciale*', '*cuvée spéciale*' or '*extra reserve*'. Ignore them for they
are all meaningless. They are just there to hype the wine.

Italy

The Italian label shows:

- ◆ 1. The vintage
- ◆ 2. The wine region and the DOCG declaration of origin. The Classico region is considered to be the best part of the Chianti region

- 3. The name of the wine
- 4. The name and address of the producer and bottler
- 5. The contents of the bottle
- 6. The alcohol content of the wine

Other words which you may find on an Italian wine label are:

- Riserva – a wine which has been specially selected and aged for at least two years
- Novello – wines which are similar to French '*nouveau*'

Spain

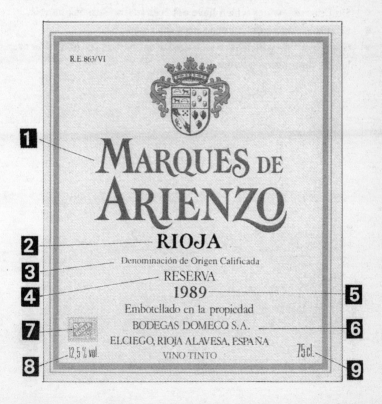

- ◆ 1. The name of the wine
- ◆ 2. The wine region
- ◆ 3. The DO declaration of origin
- ◆ 4. The quality designation. Reserva shows that the wine has been aged in barrel and bottle for longer than an ordinary Rioja
- ◆ 5. The vintage
- ◆ 6. The name and address of the producers and bottlers
- ◆ 7. The official seal of the Rioja denomination
- ◆ 7a. The alcohol content
- ◆ 8. The contents of the bottle

Other words which you might find on Spanish wine labels are:

- ◆ Sin Crianza – wines which have not been matured in oak barrels
- ◆ Crianza – wines which have seen some wood
- ◆ Gran Reserva – which have been aged in oak barrels and bottled for even longer than Reserva wines

New World

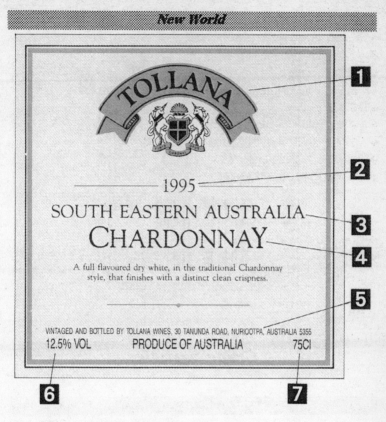

The Australian label is typical of many. It includes:

- ◆ 1. The name of the producer
- ◆ 2. The vintage
- ◆ 3. The wine-producing region
- ◆ 4. The grape variety
- ◆ 5. The name and address of the producer and bottler
- ◆ 6. The alcohol content
- ◆ 7. The contents of the bottle
- ◆ 8. The back label giving information about how the wine was made, what it tastes like and how you might serve it

Grape varieties

Wines which are made from one or two specific grape varieties and labelled as such are known as 'varietal wines'. They have been around in Europe in places such as Alsace for a very long time but they really came into their own in Australia and California.

Producers in these areas had traditionally labelled their wines with the name of the grower, their vineyard or even their home town. Others took names such as 'Chablis' and 'Burgundy', even though they had no connection at all with these European areas. All this had to change when the New World producers started to sell to Europe and so they hit on the idea of using varietal names.

Interest in grape varieties has soared as more and more wine labels carry these varietal names. Eastern Europe, southern France, Chile and South

Africa all use them. Chardonnay and Cabernet Sauvignon have emerged as the popular frontrunners, but what should you expect from Voignier, Chenin Blanc, Shiraz, Grenache and Sangiovese?

Grape varieties

Some wines are labelled by their grape variety and this can be useful in giving an indication, at least, of the kind of flavours to expect. Once you have tasted a Sauvignon Blanc from Touraine and one from California, or perhaps Australia, you will have a better idea of what to expect from bottles labelled Sauvignon Blanc in the future.

Describing the taste of a wine made from specific grape varieties is even more difficult than describing its style. Most people use comparative fruit and vegetable descriptions such as gooseberries, blackcurrants, apricots, mint, cucumber and violets. More extreme are 'sweaty saddles' and 'cat's pee', but these tend to be found in books and articles rather than on the supermarket shelves!

Of course, the wine doesn't actually taste exactly like the description, but is reminiscent of it ... though now I come to think of it some Aussie Cabernets do taste exactly like fresh blackcurrants!

On the next few pages there is information about the different kinds of tastes you can expect from wines made from different grape varieties and which regions they come from.

Grape varieties analysis

White grapes

Chardonnay

Regions: Originally from Burgundy (Chablis, Mâcon, Meursault) and Champagne but now from other regions of France such as VdP d'Oc. Chardonnay is also grown in Italy, Eastern Europe, South Africa, Chile, the USA, Australia and New Zealand.

Flavour: Usually dry, the unoaked wines vary from apple fresh to melons and tropical fruit whereas oaked wines take on a more buttery or vanilla flavour with the fruit.

Chenin Blanc

Regions: Very important in the Loire Valley and in South Africa. It is also grown in the USA, Australia and New Zealand.

Flavour: Usually dry with high acidity it can also be very sweet. Flavours vary from green apples and lemons to honey and flowers or even damp straw.

Gewürztraminer

Regions: Alsace, Germany, Eastern Europe and New Zealand. It is also grown in Australia.

Flavour: Dry, off-dry or very sweet with a flavour of lychees and roses with spicy or floral overtones.

Muscat

Regions: France, particularly Alsace and the southern Rhône, Italy where it is known as Moscato (Asti Spumante) and Spain where it is known as Moscatel. It is also grown in California, Australia and South Africa.

Flavour: Dry to very sweet indeed with a very grapey taste. Can also include apples, oranges, raisins and toffee among its flavours.

Pinot Blanc

Regions: Alsace, northern Italy where it is known as Pinot Bianco and Germany where it is known as Weissburgunder.

Flavour: Dry with apples and honey.

Pinot Gris

Regions: Alsace and Italy where it is known as Pinot Grigio.

Flavour: Dry and fairly acidic with fresh apples or lemons if it is picked young (Italy) or full and spicy and not dissimilar to Gewürztraminer (Alsace).

Riesling

Regions: This is the great grape variety of Germany, but it is also found in Alsace, Austria and other parts of Eastern Europe. However, it should not be confused with the Welschrieslings and Rizlings of Eastern Europe. It is also grown in Australia and New Zealand, where it is known as Rhine Riesling, and in California.

Flavour. Dry to very sweet. Flavours vary from grapefruit and apples to flowery, tropical fruits, petrol and raisins.

Sauvignon Blanc

Regions. The Loire Valley (Sancerre and Pouilly Fume) and Bordeaux are home to this grape variety, but is now grown extensively in New Zealand. It also appears in southern France, occasionally in Spain and Italy and in California (Fume Blanc), Chile and South Africa.

Flavour. Very dry or very sweet with flavours varying from minty herbaceous leaves to gooseberries, asparagus and elderflowers.

Semillon

Regions. Bordeaux (Sauternes and Barsac) and Australia. It is also grown in New Zealand, Chile, South Africa and California.

Flavour. Dry, medium or sweet; oaked or unoaked with a lemony and apple flavour or with peaches, pineapples and honey.

Trebbiano

Regions. This is the most widely planted white grape variety in Italy and many of the country's wines are made from it.

Flavour. Dry and fresh without much individual varietal flavour.

Voignier

Regions. Northern Rhône Valley (Condrieu) and now various parts of southern France and in Eastern Europe.

Flavour. Dry with apricots and peaches.

Red grapes

Cabernet Franc

Regions. The Loire Valley and Bordeaux, also northern Italy, California and Australia.

Flavour. Blackcurrants and stalky leaves.

Cabernet Sauvignon

Regions. Originally Bordeaux but now from the south of France, northern and central Italy, the whole of Eastern Europe, South Africa, Chile, California,

Australia and New Zealand.

Flavour. Blackcurrants in one form or another with cedarwood and tar (Bordeaux) or vanilla (oak aged New World wines).

Gamay

Regions. Beaujolais plus small quantities in the Loire Valley and in Australia.

Flavour. Light wine with cherries, strawberries and a little cabbage.

Grenache

Regions. Spain, where it is is known as Garnacha, the southern Rhône Valley and in the south of France generally. It is also grown in Australia where it is blended into a good many wines.

Flavour. Blackberries and plums.

Merlot

Regions. Bordeaux and Languedoc/Roussillon, northern Italy, Eastern Europe and Chile. A little is grown in Australia and New Zealand, but California is now planting large quantities.

Flavour. Soft blackcurrants and plums with mint.

Nebbiolo

Regions. Piedmont (Barolo).

Flavour. Complex mixed berry fruit with high wood tannins.

Pinot Noir

Regions. Originally from Burgundy but increasingly from New World countries such as California, Australia, New Zealand and Chile. It is also grown in Germany and Eastern Europe – here it is often known as Spatburgunder.

Flavour. Varies from raspberries, strawberries and beetroot when young to vegetal when mature.

Sangiovese

Regions. Tuscany and central Italy (Chianti, Brunello di Montalcino and Vino Nobile di Montepulciano). A little is now being grown in California and Australia.

Flavour. Varies from violets and cherries with herbs to vegetal tobacco.

Syrah

Regions: Northern Rhône Valley (Hermitage, Cornas, Crozes-Hermitage), Châteauneuf-du-Pape and the Midi. It is also grown in Australia where it is known as Shiraz. A small amount is also grown in California.

Flavour: Usually peppery, but may be fresh and fruity or full of mature coffee, chocolate, leather and tar.

Tempranillo

Regions: Spain (Rioja and as a single variety in wines from other regions).

Flavour: Strawberries, blackcurrants and pepper usually with a good deal of vanilla from the oak used to mature the wines in Rioja.

Zinfandel

Regions: This is California's own grape variety. As well as making red wines of all kinds it is also used to make "blush" wines.

Flavour: May be fresh and very fruity with mixed red berry fruits or may be heavier with more vegetal and woody flavours.

Vintages

The vintage is the year that the grapes were harvested and made into wine. In some years the growing conditions are particularly good and the very best wines are produced. In others, conditions are poor and it is difficult to make good wine.

Vintage charts attempt to assess the quality of wines produced in a given year. Vintages are often more important in Europe than they are in Australia or California, for there is much greater variation in the weather conditions in Europe.

But just how important are vintages? The answer is: not very important at the table wine level or for branded wines (they don't usually carry a date anyway). These wines will often be blends designed to eradicate the vagaries of the weather.

Even at the Vin de Pays or country wine level the vintage is not all that important. These wines are made to be drunk young and though you may detect a slight difference from year to year, no-one is planning to keep them.

At the Appellation Contrôlée level the vintage must be stated on the bottle. For us high street wine buyers this can be useful, but not critical. If you read that your favourite Loire wines have done badly one year, you may switch to Vin de Pays d'Oc, Pinot Grigio or La Mancha for a while.

Equally, a series of good vintages in Bordeaux, for example, will mean that quality wine will be available even at the lowest levels. You may therefore decide that it is worth buying in a stock of your favourite claret to keep for a year or two.

However, it is really only if you are thinking of buying some older vintages (very expensive even if you can find them), or planning to buy wine *en primeur* (before it has been bottled) and keep it for a few years that vintages become really important. If you are going to spend a large sum investing in wine, it makes sense to start with the best years.

Red wines worth keeping:
Good Bordeaux wines
Burgundy at the 'Village' level and upwards
Rhône wines such as Crozes-Hermitage, Hermitage, Côte Rotie and Châteauneuf-du-Pape
Chianti Classico Reserva from Tuscany and Barolo from Piedmont
Rioja Crianza Reserva and Grand Reserva from Spain
Some New World wines from California and Australia will also improve with a year or two in bottle

White wines worth keeping:
White Burgundy (Meursault and Montrachet and even Chablis), Sauternes, Barsac and Premières Côtes de Bordeaux
German Rieslings at the Auslese level and upwards
Vintage Champagne (even non-vintage Champagne can improve for a year or two)

Judging the vintage

The problem now arises of deciding which *is* a good vintage. Reports pour out of the various wine-growing regions during the year, culminating in a positive deluge at and after the harvest. The problem is that according to these no region has a *very* bad vintage. You will also find that every grower believes that his neighbours have had a much worse time than he had!

Independent reports from journalists and the like are not all that much better, though a year hailed as 'the vintage of the century' (a common occurrence these days) will probably end up being quite good. The point which is often forgotten is that the wine goes on developing and maturing until it is drunk and some years which have been written off by the pundits produce very pleasant wines eight or ten years later.

The other problem is that vintage assessments are far too general. They can only give a broad indication of the *average* level of quality. Individual wines may be much better or much worse and you really need to know your grower for detailed assessment.

Levels of alcohol

Other useful information can come from the stated alcohol levels. Light wines like those from Germany, come in at the 8–9.5% alcohol by volume level, whereas some of the red wines of Italy reach 13.5–14% levels. Obviously the latter will need a fair amount of food to offset the alcohol alone.

Wines which are high in alcohol are often very full-bodied with lots of fruit extract and high levels of tannin. Some of them can be very overpowering.

Back labels

Look to see if the bottle has a back label as well as the official front label. These potentially helpful notes first appeared on wines from California and Australia. The better ones tell you about the grape varieties used and the resultant style of the wine and how tannic, acid or oaky it is. They often include helpful serving suggestions as well.

Most of the supermarkets have cleverly taken up the idea for their own-label wines and produce back labels which are both informative and easy to understand. If you are not sure of the meaning of some of the descriptions, have a look at the list of common descriptions on pages 206 – 208.

Shelf descriptions

Some taste attributes of the wine, such as how dry or how sweet it is and how much body it has, are not always shown on the label.

The level of sweetness is one of the most important flavour characteristics of a wine and you probably have a very definite idea of how dry or how sweet you like your wine to be. You may also know that Muscadet and Chablis are pretty dry and that Liebfraumilch and Lambrusco are on the sweet side. But do you know exactly where Bulgarian Misket, South African Colombard, Australian Rhine Riesling or Chilean Chardonnay come on the sweetness/ dryness scale?

Sweetness guide for white and rosé wines

To save you having to remember exactly where each wine comes in relation to another, a guide has been drawn up to indicate the sweetness levels of white wines. It is based on a simple nine-point scale with 1 as very dry and 9 as very sweet (see page 12).

Most supermarkets and off-licence chains show these symbols and numbers on their shelf descriptions. Use them to find your way around areas which are new to you or in experimenting with different wines. Don't just stick at the same sweetness level – try wines from some of the other levels as well. This advice refers as much to those who usually buy at number 1 on the scale as to those who buy at numbers 4 or 5. Most of us become rather blinkered in our choice of wine.

There seems to be a view that dry white wine is the most sophisticated and the best choice. People who like sweeter wines are made to feel that they should apologise for their tastes. This is quite wrong. It is just not true to say that dry is best. It depends on the individual wine concerned. Some dry white wines are astringent and unpleasant and if you strike one of these in your first foray into drier wines, it will not be surprising that you are put off. Conversely there are some sweet wines which do not have enough acidity to offset the sugar and these can be quite cloying and unpleasant. However, there are first-class wines at all levels of the scale and the dry-wine snob is losing out on a fair amount of enjoyment. So keep an open mind and drink around!

The taste guide for red wines

This guide endeavours to assess the total taste experience of red wines. It uses a simple five-point alphabetical scale of A to E. (See page 13.) At A the wines are undemanding and easy to drink. As you move through the scale the wines become fuller and deeper with more concentrated flavours, so at E the wines are fairly heavy and with quite a distinctive taste. They often have high levels of alcohol and tannin.

This guide is not as widely accepted as the sweetness guide though some stores do use it. The problem is that wines from a particular area can vary a good deal so they cannot just be lumped into a category on the basis of origin. Thus a Rioja at one store may fall into a different category to that at another.

Wine language

Many supermarkets and off-licence chains are making great efforts to increase the flow of information on wine. There are short descriptions on the shelves above or below the wine racks and supermarkets and off-licence chains often also produce wine lists and booklets describing the wines.

The language used is fairly straightforward and is aimed at giving a description of the style of the wine in the bottle. It is designed to help you decide whether a particular wine will make light and easy-drinking at a summer party or will be better suited to drinking with your favourite casserole on a cold winter's night.

A guide to the meaning of common descriptions

◆ **Acidity:** This gives zest and freshness to a wine and helps to balance sweeter wines which would just be cloying without it. It sometimes tastes rather like raw cooking apples, at others more like lemon or grapefruit juice. Too much acidity is unpleasant.

◆ **Aromatic:** A generally fragrant or spicy aroma.

◆ **Baked:** A 'hot' rather jammy or earthy smell or taste produced when the grapes have been grown in excessive sunshine with low rainfall.

◆ **Balance:** This is the very important ratio between all the different characteristics of the wine, such as fruit, acidity, tannin and alcohol. These should all harmonise to give a rounded effect.

◆ **Barrel-aged:** This refers to the fact that the wine has spent some time in oak barrels. Maturing wine in oak adds to the complexity of the taste as the wine will take up some flavours from the wood.

◆ **Body:** This refers to the feel of the wine in the mouth due both to the fullness of flavour and the level of alcohol. It may be described as light or full.

◆ **Character:** This indicates that the wine has a distinctive style to it.

◆ **Closed:** This is a wine which does not smell or taste as much as you would expect. It may not be mature enough.

◆ **Complex:** A wine with many facets.

◆ **Crisp:** Often a euphemism for very acidic.

◆ **Elegant:** A stylish and refined quality; the opposite of opulent.

◆ **Flowery:** This usually means the wine has a fragrant, perfumed and flower-like aroma and flavour.

◆ **Fresh:** This is a wine which retains its youthful acidity.

◆ **Fruity:** This overworked word refers to the prominent flavour of the grapes, but it does not necessarily mean grapey as in the flavour of fresh table grapes.

◆ **Honeyed:** This is a characteristic of some white wines and is often intensified with age.

◆ **Mellow or mature:** A wine which has losts all its sharp edges and is well rounded.

◆ **Noble rot:** Grapes which have been attacked with a particular kind of mould will shrivel up and their juice will concentrate. Wine made from these grapes has a very distinctive aroma and taste which is sought after in sweet wines.

◆ **Oaky:** This is a flavour imparted to the wine from ageing in oak barrels. It can have a distinctive vanilla-like smell.

◆ **Petillant:** This is a very slight degree of natural sparkle. It shows as tiny bubbles on the side of the glass and a faint prickle on the tongue.

◆ **Rich:** A full-bodied wine with plenty of fruit extract.

◆ **Soft:** This usually means that the acidity levels of the wine are quite low.

◆ **Sur lie:** This is the phrase used to describe wine which has been allowed to mature on its own sediment.

◆ **Tannin:** This gives a furry, rather harsh impression on the gums and teeth. Some tannin can be very pleasant, too much is not. A tannic wine may soften with age.

And finally a couple of words which you are unlikely to find on a wine list, but which it may be useful to know:

◆ **Corked:** This does not mean that there are bits of crumbled cork in the wine, but refers to wine which has a very distinctive smell and taste of mould or decaying wood. It is caused by a fungal infection of the cork.

◆ **Oxidised or maderised:** These terms refer to wine which has been spoilt by exposure to air. The latter term is used more often in connection with white wine. The wine has a characteristic slightly sherry-like taste and a darker than usual colour.

Branded wines

These are wines which are likely to taste the same from year to year. They are designed to do so. Having achieved this the wine-maker then proceeds to advertise the brand so that when we walk into a wine store, there will be at least one or two wines we know.

This is not necessarily to be condenmed. Most of the branded wines are well made, even if they are sweeter than the connoisseur's choice and rather more expensive than similar wines which are not branded.

Everyone knows, I think, that Blue Nun is a blended Liebfraumilch and those who buy it know what to expect and will not be disappointed. It is a safe buy. Sichel, the makers of Blue Nun, have spent a lot of money ensuring that it will be so. The quality of the grapes used is very high and the quality control extremely sophisticated.

Piat d'Or and Mouton Cadet operate on the same principle. If you are in a crowded shops when the assistants have no time to help you or you are wading through a badly-designed wine list in a restaurant, the familiar name will come to your rescue.

However, you should be aware that you are paying for this peace of mind. Advertising and clever marketing costs money and that expense will certainly be passed on to you, the buyer. Nor should you believe all that the ads tell you. The ads for one of these well-known brands would have you believe that in France that particular wine is a French favourite. In fact I saw it in a Calais supermarket displayed under the sign 'Vins Sans Frontiers' with a small collection of wines from outside France!

So, my advice is to buy a branded wine you know and like if you are in a hurry, but when you have a little time to spare to talk to the shop assistant or to browse along the labels make the effort to try something else in the same price range. You will probably get a much more interesting wine.

Boxes, tins and cartons

Modern packaging methods are here to stay and they have their uses. Canned wine is handy when on a picnic or snacking away from home. The wine does not seem to suffer from contact with the tin's lining and the quality is acceptable. Rather more attractive are the small glass bottles holding 250cl which are just begining to appear in the supermarkets.

Cartons are less popular then they used to be. They are difficult to open and to pour. And you cannot re-close them if you don't drink up all the contents.

Wine boxes, on the other hand, are very useful for parties and for people who only want to drink a glass or two at a time, but like to have a supply on hand. When wine boxes were first introduced it was often thought that the wine was cheaper. In fact, a comparison with the same wine in the bottle often shows that you are paying about the same, volume for volume.

And the wine does not keep for ever. A few weeks really is the maximum time you should keep the wine after the carton box has been opened. Take care when fiddling with the tap – this is where air can start to creep in.

The wine in wine boxes is variable. Some of it is pretty ordinary, and some is very good. To help you to choose there are comparative tasting notes on some of the supermarket wine boxes on pages 177–187.

Low-alcohol and fruit wines

'Reduced alcohol' and 'low-alcohol' wines do not have any accurate definitions. The wine might contain anything from 0.5 to 5.5% alcohol (normal wine being around 8–13%).

If you are planning to buy one of these products it is obviously important to read the small print on the label where the actual alcoholic content is given. Remember that 'low-alcohol wine' at 5.5% contains more alcohol than some beers and lagers.

No- and low-alcohol wines are obviously an attractive idea but are they an attractive buy? From a purely economic point of view the answer is yes. They are now cheaper than real wine. The excise duty that they used to attract has been lowered to rates more proportional to their alcohol content. Alcohol-free wines do not command any duty at all.

But what of the taste? Sadly these wines simply do not have the same aroma and flavour as real wine. Whether the wine is dealcoholised by heat treatment, centrifusion, reverse osmosis, arrested fermentation or dilution (usually with fruit juices), a good deal is lost in the process.

On the whole I would recommend anyone who wants to cut down on their alcohol intake to drink fewer (and maybe better?) glasses of wine or to add some sparkling water to the wine and revive the old custom of making 'spritzers. If you want to cut out alcohol altogether drink fruit juice.

The choice of so-called 'fruit' wines expanded rapidly a few years ago but the boom is now over and alcoholic lemonade and the like have become more popular. The few that remain may come in at anything from 3% alcohol by volume to as much as 7.5%. So once again it is important to read the label carefully.

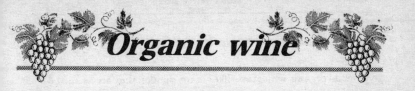

Organic wine

*T*he idea of a 'green' approach to the environment has taken a strong hold in the fields of packaging, domestic appliances and even food. But wine has largely escaped the trend. As yet the demand for ingredients or additive labelling is not very strong but there are demands for sulphur levels to be indicated. Given the EU food legislation it can only be a matter of time before such labelling is introduced.

In the meantime those who are interested in all things organic can now find wines which should come within their framework. There are around seven companies specialising in importing organic wines and some of the supermarkets, strongly led by Safeway, are also endeavouring to offer an organic choice on their wine shelves.

The idea of growing vines organically, without the use of chemical fertilisers and pesticides, is catching on with some growers, even more than it has with their customers. France leads the field, closely followed by Germany and Italy. Spain and Portugal are just not interested. A few excellent organic wines are also coming in from New Zealand, Australia and California.

The correct EU terminology for organic wine is 'wine made from organically grown grapes'. This is because the current regulations only refer to the cultivation of grapes not to their vinification. However, it looks as if the term 'organic wine' will remain if it is explained somewhere on the label.

The line between organic and the best of the rest has been blurred to say the least and it will probably remain that way despite the regulations. There are plenty of ecologically sound vineyards, where artificial help is kept to a minimum and where the wines are naturally stable.

On the other hand organic producers are still able to use sulphur. The levels are kept to a minimum so if you are asthmatic or sensitive to sulphur it could be worth paying extra for organic wine.

It is likely that you *will* have to pay more for organic wines. The organic wine-maker has a hard task. He is attempting to make modern wines for modern tastes without the benefit of modern chemicals. This can be both labour-intensive and extremely chancy.

What do organic wines taste like?

So what do organic wines taste like? In my opinion they are as 'mixed a bag' as any group of wines. I have had some very poor organic wines and some very odd ones. Some have made me question my ideas of what a wine from a particular area should taste like. However, I have also had some first-class organic wines which seemed to have extracted even more wonderful fruit flavours than are usually encountered in first-class wine.

Like all wine, it's a case of try it and see. A good opportunity to do just that is at the Organic Wine Fair held at Ryton Gardens in England every July.

Here are some addresses and telephone numbers of wine merchants specialising in organic wines:

◆   Haughton Agencies, Sole Bay Brewery, Southwold, Suffolk, IP18 6JW. Tel:01502 727288. Fax:01502 727289.

◆   HDRA, National Centre for Organic Gardening, Ryton-on-Dunsmore, Coventry CV8 3LG. Tel:01203 303517. Fax:01203 639229.

◆   The Organic Wine Company, PO Box 81, High Wycombe, Bucks HP13 5QN. Tel:01494 446557. Fax:01494 713030.

◆   Real Foods Ltd, 37 Broughton St., Edinburgh EH1 3JU. Tel:0131 557 1911. Fax:0131 5583530.

◆   Rodgers Fine Wines, 37 Ben Bank Rd, Silkstone Common, Barnsley, South Yorks S75 4PE. Tel:01226 790794. (German Wine Specialist.)

◆   Vinceremos Wines, 261 Upper Town St., Bramley, Leeds, W. Yorks LS13 3JJ. Tel:01132 577545. Fax:01132 576906.

◆   Vintage Roots, Sheeplands Farm, Wargrave Rd, Wargrave, Berks RG10 8DT. Tel:01734 401222. Fax:01734 404814.

Some of the supermarkets and high street off-licence chains are also starting to offer organic wines. Safeway, for example, has a range of ten such wines. Some organic wines have been included in the listings on pages 14 to 187.

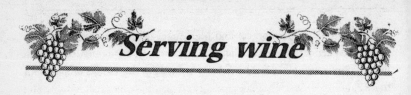

Serving wine

Opening wine

The corkscrew

*S*tart with a good corkscrew and most problems will be avoided. Choose one with a wide spiral that ends in a curved, not straight, point. A Brabantia or Screwpull are both excellent for all corks, but essential for long corks such as those used in fine wines and vintage port. A 'waiter's friend' (the type used by wine waiters) is good for everyday use. The double lever type is fine too, if it has a curved end.

Curly-ended corkscrews help to stop little bits of cork falling into the wine when it is opened. Sometimes the cork is so crumbly that it partially breaks up. This doesn't affect the wine. You can either pick out the pieces or sieve the wine into a flask or decanter.

Some cheaper bottles of wine now have artificial corks. They can be pulled in just the same way as real corks but they will not crumble so the type of corkscrew is less critical.

The capsule

There's no special skill in opening a bottle of wine, but you should either remove the capsule which covers the top of the neck altogether or cut it round so that it is clear of the lip. This is particularly important if it is made of lead, though lead capsules are gradually disappearing. Some people like to leave the lower part of the capsule in place so that if the bottle touches the rim of the glass, the impact is softened.

Next wipe the top of the bottle with a damp cloth to remove any dirt or moulds (harmless) which have grown under the capsule. Insert the corkscrew and remove the cork. Wipe the rim again and pour.

Corked wine

Very occasionally corks are infected with a fungal growth which makes both the cork and the wine smell very mouldy. This is known as corked wine and it should not be drunk.

Return the bottle and the cork to the shop where it was bought. There is no obligation to replace it, but reputable shops want to know if their wine is corked so that they can alert the original supplier and, nine times out of ten, they will replace the bottle for you.

This problem seems to be on the increase and has been the incentive behind the introduction of artificial corks. These corks do not allow any air to get to the wine and so far are only used with cheaper wines which would not be expected to mature in the bottle and which should be drunk a year or so after they are made.

Sparkling wine

Opening bottles of Champagne or sparkling wine does require a little more care and skill. Corks have been known to fly out the moment the pressure of the wire cage is removed and if the bottle is pointing at your face, or at other people's, the result can be disastrous. So, keep a firm thumb on the top of the cork as you remove it and ease the cork out slowly and carefully. (There's no need to make a huge pop!) Keep the bottle pointing at the ceiling.

To decant or not?

None of the wine recommended in this book is likely to need decanting. Only fine clarets and vintage ports throw a sediment these days. All other wines are either too young to have developed any or are so well filtered that even ten or twelve years in a bottle does not mean that any sediment will result.

If you do buy or are given a fine claret or port, decant by very carefully pouring the wine from the bottle into the decanter in one continuous movement. Forget the candle, and position a bright light such as a torch or an unshaded lamp bulb behind the bottle so that you can see when the sediment reaches the neck. Stop pouring. Use the small amount of wine left in the bottle to enhance the sauce or gravy you are serving with the main course!

There are other reasons for decanting wines, however. You may have a fine glass decanter which you want to show off, or you may not want your guests to see the label or the bottle.

You may also want the air to get to the wine to allow it to take up the oxygen (breathe) and so age quickly. Test this for yourself by experimenting with a bottle of good Chianti. Decant it and try it when you open it, an hour after that, and then after another hour. Try it again the next day and you will see what happens to it. Remember to agitate the decanter before pouring as the top layer of liquid nearest to the air will oxidise before the rest.

Generally speaking, wines which are almost but not quite ready to drink will benefit the most from a little air. If the wine is very young, decanting the wine, even an hour or two before it is to be served, will not bring it to the level of maturity it would get with time. Wines which are a little too old will oxidise quickly and spoil.

Decanting is also wasted on wines which do not have any ageing potential at all. So don't try it with white wines, Vin de Pays wines, Valpolicella and Beaujolais.

The French, who have very definite ideas about these things, believe that the glass is decanter enough. If you think your wine needs improving after you pour it, you can deliberately aerate it by swishing it round the glass for a moment before you drink it.

Temperature control

Serve white wine at cellar temperature and red wine at room temperature. This is the traditional advice, but who has a wine cellar these days to check on the temperature? An hour in the fridge is probably more useful advice today. White wine should not be overchilled. This is particularly important for those fresh, dry wines costing under £3 a bottle. There will be nothing left to taste if they are too cold!

Room temperature creates another problem. In the days when there was no central heating, room temperature was lower than it is today! Red wine should be served at around 15°C, give or take a degree. So, check the temperature of the spare room and keep your bottles in there! If your wine is too cold, don't put it by the radiator – only one side will heat up (or overheat). Better to plunge the bottle into warm water for a *very* short time.

Some red wines, such as Beaujolais and Bardolino, are very good served chilled. Try it in summer.

Ideally, wine should be served at approximately the following temperatures:

Mature red wines	15–17°C
Young red wines and country wines	13–16°C
Beaujolais and Valpolicella	10–11°C
Sherry	10°C
Champagne and dry white wines	9–11°C
Sweet white wines	6–7°C

Glasses

The glass you drink out of does affect your appreciation. Think of that good bottle of Chablis you drank out of the plastic mugs last summer. Did it taste the same as usual? So, don't just use any old glass.

Simple Paris goblets are just about OK, but try using glasses where the shape of the upper space funnels slightly inwards. This channels the aroma and bouquet towards the nose and helps you to enjoy both the smell and the taste of the wine.

Don't give way to custom and fill the glass completely full. It is not mean to leave a space at the top of the glass – this is done to enjoy the aroma.

Sparkling wine is best served in slightly tall or fluted glasses to charm the bubble up in long attractive trails. Old-fashioned saucer-shaped glasses dissipate the bubbles and are easy to spill. They are best kept for ice-cream sundaes.

Short-term storage

If you haven't finished all the wine in the bottle, you can simply re-cork. Avoid the temptation to turn the cork upside down. It's easier to push back in this way, but you could be adding a cocktail of nasty bacteria or moulds. You might cut the end off first and then replace. Place the bottle in the fridge and drink the next day.

It's a better idea to invest in one of the proprietary bottle stoppers. Some are better than others, but people tend not to agree on about this. I use the pump-out-air or vacuum type and find it very satisfactory, but there are gas types as well.

If you have bought in wine for a party, store it in the coolest room in the house. Weekend stocks for the following week will be perfectly all right in the kitchen, but do lay the bottles on their sides to stop corks drying out.

Thinking about a cellar

The word 'cellar' may seem too grandiose a word to describe the space in which most of us keep surplus stocks of wine. But whatever its shape, size or location (even the kitchen), a stock of wine for future drinking is, indeed, a cellar.

It's quite sensible to buy in stocks of wine, even if you are paying less than £5 a bottle. First of all, you have wines on hand to offer to unexpected visitors. You can also build up a selection of wine so that you have a choice of what to serve when you have friends for supper or are catering for a special anniversary.

Even more importantly, quite a lot of wines improve with as little as six months' or a year's extra bottle age. Phrases like 'still very young', 'full of promise' and 'will benefit if kept' appear in both supermarket and wine shop literature and point the way. You could also save a little money by buying the wines when you first see them. Prices could rise or you may not be able to find the same vintage in a year or two.

Having bought yourself several bottles or even a case or two of wine you will need to store them. Most homes reveal one or two areas which can be pressed into service as a cellar. Try the cupboard under the stairs, the spare room, the back of a wardrobe or an old freezer cabinet in the garage. At a pinch, a corner of the living room or the kitchen will do. Place racks away from appliances which give off heat (i.e. the fridge and freezer as well as the cooker).

Here is a checklist for any prospective cellar:

◆ Use a wooden or wire rack if you can. However, cases of wine with proper compartments can be turned on their sides and be used and re-used for a time. Remember always to take the wine from the top first. The cardboard sections are rarely strong enough if unsupported by the bottle below.

◆ If possible keep your store of wine in the dark. Lay the bottles on their sides to prevent the corks drying out.

◆ Try to find an area where the temperature does not change too rapidly from hot to cold or vice versa. This is more important than keeping the wine at the ideal temperature of 12°C. If you do get temperature changes the wine will age more quickly. White wine may throw a sediment of crystals in very cold weather, but it only means that the wine has not been centrifuged to death and it won't affect the taste of the wine.

◆ Avoid damp or airless positions. However, the former can be alleviated with the use of damp crystals.

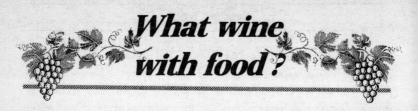

What wine with food?

*W*ine and food are natural partners. But should you be drinking particular wines with particular foods? The enthusiastic 'foodie' will probably say yes. But in most cases the wines you fancy will go with the foods you like.

It is true that some partnerships work better than others and in an ideal world the wine and food should so enhance each other that both are improved. But most of us do not have the time or the wine stocks to make the ideal match at every meal. Instead, we have to consider whether the chilli con carne will swamp our best wine or whether the plate of salami and olives needs a wine with plenty of acidity.

In the days of elaborate four-, five- and six- course dinners, rules were developed about what wines went with which food. White wine partnered the fish course and red wine went with the meat course.

Today, meals are simpler and most people are unlikely to serve more than one wine at a meal, unless it is a very special occasion. So, the chosen wine has to cope with very much more than it would have done before.

And if there are rules, we know that they are there to be broken. After all, the French, Spanish and Italians all cook fish in red wine and serve sweet wine with rich pâtés and blue cheeses.

Where do you start?

There are so many wines to choose from and so many different ways of serving simple food that any kind of analysis seems fraught with difficulty.

However, here are some questions you could ask yourself to help sort things out to start with:

Is the dish plainly cooked? If it is, it will probably show off your best wines very well. The food and wine will not be fighting for attention and the flavour of the wine will not be swamped.

Is the main ingredient or the dish itself a fairly fatty or oily one? Good acidity in the wine is the answer here. Italian wines are often thought to be very acidic, but they are specifically designed to partner the rich Italian cuisine.

Is the dish particularly strongly flavoured or spicy? Here you have a choice: one answer is to choose a full rich wine, hopefully with complementary flavours; the other is to retreat into a fresh but simple wine which will allow the food to shine.

Does the dish have sweet or fruit flavours of its own? If it does, you should choose a slightly sweeter wine. Completely dry wines can taste very astringent when there is sugar present in the meal. Sometimes you are able to match the fruity flavours in the wine with those of the dish.

Does the dish have a well-flavoured sauce? Wines with a lower level of tannin, such as Burgundy, tend to go better with sauces than do the tannic wines of Bordeaux, Piedmont or Tuscany.

What are the component flavours of the dish? Here you can start to try and match the flavours with those you find in different wines.

It is possible to go on analysing combinations to the nth degree and still end up arguing whether a German Riesling Spätlese from the Rheingau partnered your smoked salmon roulade with smoked trout mousse better than an Alsace Gewürztraminer, or an aged Coteaux du Layon Chenin Blanc! At the end of the day it's all pretty subjective.

So what follows is only my own broad guidelines for matching wines to the main dish of the meal, or to special types of meals, such as barbecues, take-aways and picnics.

I hope that the ideas will serve as a starting point for anyone who wants to widen the range of wines which they serve at home and that it will encourage lots of experimentation and discussion!

Food and wine partnerships

In no particular order:

Take-away meals

◆ **Chinese:** Red wines are not brilliant with Chinese food though I think you can just about get away with Beaujolais or a red wine from the Loire such as Chinon or Saumur Champigny. These can be very good with crispy duck. However, a fresh rosé is often a better choice for dishes with sauces. If you prefer white wine, try any Riesling wine: dry from Alsace, medium dry from Germany. Australian Rhine Riesling works well with rich sauces and German Halbtrocken wines with deep fried food and dim sum.

◆ **Indian:** The wine nearly always comes off second best here, so a fresh and light red or white will probably do. Listel Gris is good with curried fish and Gewürztraminer with tandoori dishes. Australian Shiraz may also take the curry head on. Otherwise, stick to simple Eastern European Cabernet Sauvignon or Beaujolais.

◆ **Mexican:** All that chilli is even more of a problem. Stick to wines in the light and fresh categories. You could also drink up wines which you have found to be too astringent. The chilli seems to kill the acidity and what fruit there is in the wine comes through!

◆ **Fish and chips:** Fresh light wines with good acidity are needed to cut through the rich batter. Try white Vins de Pays wines, Muscadet or Pinot Grigio, or if you like a stronger flavour, one of the Sauvignon wines from Hungary, the Czech Republic, the Loire or Bordeaux. (*See also* Fishy Feasts.) For something a touch sweeter try the Bulgarian Country whites.

◆ **Pizza-to-go:** For the reds, choose from the light or medium-bodied Vin de Pays from southern France, Chianti or Montepulciano d'Abruzzo. Try one of the fuller-flavoured whites from the New World to match the tomato and herbs or a dry Italian white from the Veneto or Trentino to cope with rich toppings.

◆ **Hamburgers:** Good straightforward Bulgarian Cabernet Sauvignon is an excellent choice here. Or if you want to splash out a bit more, try an Australian Cabernet Sauvignon.

◆ **Barbecues:** If it's to be a barbecue party, go for one of the party wines from the listings section of this book. Fresh and light Vin de Pays and Eastern European reds work well too. If it's a more serious meal, then choose from the medium-bodied reds for plain grills and from the fuller-flavoured reds and whites for marinated and basted dishes. Favourites are Chianti with herby sausages, Chilean Merlot with spicy chicken drumsticks and Australian Cabernet/Shiraz with barbecued spare-ribs.

Roast dinners

◆ **Meat:** Simple roast beef, lamb and pork all show off good wines. Claret is traditional with roast beef, but any of the wines in the medium-bodied red section or full-flavoured whites should be good. Lamb needs something a little lighter so try a Beaujolais, Zinfandel or a red wine like Chinon from the Loire Valley.

◆ **Chicken:** Almost any wine works well with roast chicken, though those in the fuller-bodied red section could be a bit overpowering. If the chicken is served in a sauce, choose a fruity wine which will complement the flavours of the sauce. Match the tropical fruity flavours of an Australian Semillon or Semillon/Chardonnay with chicken in tomato sauce or serve a spicy Gewürztraminer with chicken chasseur.

◆ **Duck:** Duck can be a bit fatty and so an element of acidity is needed. The tannin in red wine does not go well with duck, so try a fruity wine such as Beaujolais, Zinfandel or a light red Vin de Pays. White wines from the Loire, like Vouvray, are good with duck, or for something rather different try an oaky New World Chardonnay.

◆ **Game:** This is always a rich meat and the fuller-bodied flavoured wines are best. Try Syrah-based wines from the Rhône or Shiraz from Australia, Rioja or one of the Portuguese wines, such as Bairrada or Alentejo. White wine lovers should try a German Auslese medium dry wine.

Christmas dinners

◆ **Turkey:** Like chicken, this meat is very easy to match. It will be the stuffing or the accompaniments which may swing the choice to or from a particular style. New World Chardonnay goes well with turkey, but claret is the classic choice.

◆ **Goose:** This is not nearly as fatty when it is cooked as everyone seems to think, but it is well-flavoured. Try Pinot Gris/Tokai or Gewürztraminer from Alsace, or an Auslese Riesling from Germany. Good reds include Fitou, full-bodied Côte du Rhône or Australian Cabernet Shiraz.

Fishy feasts

The combination of red wine and white fish can leave a kind of metallic flavour in the mouth. This is worse with more tannic wines than with fresh and fruity ones. The lighter Vin de Pays, Beaujolais, Hungarian Merlot-based wines, Loire reds and Bardolino are all worth trying with well-flavoured fish like salmon, char-grilled or fried fish, or with fish stews and casseroles.

Most white wines in the fresh and light category will go well with fish and with shellfish. Don't forget the German Trocken wines here. The fuller-flavoured Chardonnay-based wines will go well with fish in rich sauces.

Vegetarian food

At first glance, vegetarian food seems quite easy to match to wine and, with the exception of some very strongly-flavoured ones (parsnips, asparagus and turnips), vegetables do not pose too much of a problem. But, real vegetarian food is not just vegetables. There are sauces and flavour combinations which need to be taken into account and vegetarians will need to think about the wines to match their food in much the same way as meat eaters. Try Montepulciano d'Abruzzo with vegetarian lasagne, Hungarian Chardonnay with tofu and mushroom kebabs, and a light red Spanish wine such as La Mancha with tortilla.

Really keen vegetarians may want to ensure that their wines are fully vegetarian too. Some substances used to clear wine may be of animal origin, though non-animal-based bentonite and egg whites are also used. This kind of information is not given on the label and you will have to enquire from your supplier.

Some stores such as Safeway and the Co-op offer vegetarian wines which are labelled as such.

Popular classics

Here are a few of the combinations I have found successful in the last year:

◆ **Fried chicken in a basket:** Italian Rosso Conero, light Chianti or red or white French Vin de Pays.

◆ **Chicken in cream sauce:** German Riesling Kabinett, Hungarian or Italian Chardonnay or Alsace Pinot Blanc or Hungarian Merlot.

◆ **Chicken Kiev:** Touraine Sauvignon, Orvieto, or Vin de Pays des Côtes de Gascogne or Bulgarian Country wine.

◆ **Coq au vin:** Chianti Classico, Australian Semillon/Chardonnay or Claret.

◆ **Duck a l'orange:** Beaujolais, Vouvray or a German Kabinett.

◆ **Guinea fowl with sun-dried tomatoes:** Montepulciano d'Abruzzo, Californian Dry Red, Moldovan Chardonnay.

◆ **Pasta with tomato, basil and ham sauce:** Toreldego Rotaliano, Montepulciano d'Abruzzo, Zinfandel.

◆ **Lasagne:** Pinot Grigio, Bianca di Custoza or Chilean Chardonnay.

◆ **Quiche:** Vins de Pays des Côtes de Gascogne, Alsace Pinot Blanc, red Bergerac or a Claret.

◆ **Satay with peanut sauce:** Australian Cabernet Shiraz or a good but not too assertive Sauvignon Blanc from Bordeaux, Chile or the Loire.

◆ **Pork stir-fry with mixed vegetables:** Australian Chardonnay or Cabernet/Shiraz.

◆ **Pork wiener schnitzel:** Bardolino, Barbera d'Asti, Muscadet or Italian Chardonnay.

◆ **Shepherd's pie:** Any red or white Vins de Pays or an Eastern European or Chilean Merlot or Cabernet Sauvignon.

◆ **Moussaka:** Bulgarian Cabernet Sauvignon or Chianti.

◆ **Chilli con carne:** Bardolino, most red or white Vin de Pays or a Hungarian Cabernet Sauvignon.

◆ **Steak au poivre:** Red Bergerac, Minervois or a Chianti.

Some foods are notoriously difficult to match:

◆ Vinegar in pickles or in salad dressings kills the taste of good wine.

◆ Chocolate is so rich that even the sweetest wines tend to fade before it.

◆ Eggs are perhaps better served with white wine as they may affect the taste of red wine. However, the Burgundians poach their eggs in red wine.

Cheese-board

Do you serve the cheese-board before or after the dessert? Sometimes a matter of national pride, sometimes a matter of habit, the answer may well determine the choice of wine.

If you have moved from the savoury main course through a sweet dessert to the cheese-board, you won't want to go back to an unfortified red wine. It will taste very harsh and dry after the sweetness of the dessert. This way of ordering the meal prevailed at English dinner parties and port was an obvious choice and very good it is too, but there are alternatives. Sweet white wine can go very well with blue cheese. Try it for yourself if you don't believe me. Combinations to try include Première Côte Bordeaux with blue brie, dolcelatte with Ste-Croix-du-Mont, or Stilton with Sauternes or Barsac.

In France, the cheese is traditionally served after the main course and before the dessert. This makes sense to the thrifty French mind. You do not need to introduce another wine if you don't want to – simply go on drinking the red wine already on the table. Any adjustment can come in the choice of cheese to be served.

A mixed cheese-board, so beloved of the dinner party hostess, is not a particularly good idea. Apart from the fact that you will inevitably be left with a fridge full of little bits of cheese for which you have no immediate use – you will also have to match the wine to the mildest cheese on the board.

A much better idea is to serve one cheese which will really complement the wine you are drinking. This can be red or white. In fact, some cheese tastes much better with white wine. Soft creamy cheeses, such as brie and Camembert, are delicious with good Chardonnays (both Old and New World) and goat's cheese is good with Sauvignon.

Goat's cheese will also stand up to the tannin in heavier red wines, such as Châteauneuf-du-Pape, Rioja and some Australian reds. The tannin in these wines can be a problem with milder cow's milk cheese.

Light Vin de Pays wines, Beaujolais, Valpolicella and Bardolino are good choices for almost all cheeses. Another good idea is to choose wine and cheese from the same country or area. Ideas include Chianti with pecorino, Haute Côtes de Nuits with cendre, or Barbaresco with Gorgonzola.

Wine as an aperitif

Fortified wines like sherry, white port and vermouth were the original aperitifs but table wines can also be served before the meal. Champagne or sparkling wines are a good example of this and they give a lift to a special occasions.

Off-dry wines such as French Vouvray, Australian Rhine Riesling and German Spätlese, too, are very good served at this time. If you take care in choosing the food you can continue to serve these sweeter wines through the first, and possibly, the second course of the meal. Liver pâté, for example, goes very well with slightly sweeter wine.

Tasting and assessing wine

D espite the flowery language of some wine experts, all you really need to taste and assess wine is your own sense of sight, smell and taste – plus a little practice. After all, you can certainly tell a wine you don't like from one that you do and a wine which tastes good is good!

Most people just assume that because they don't know a great deal about wine and haven't made a conscious effort to try and remember the tastes of the wines which they like, they will be unable to make any real judgements. Not so.

Of course it is useful to have a little more knowledge about the sort of factors to look out for, but practice is even more important. If you make a point of thinking about the wine you are about to drink, smell it, taste it and make a mental note, you will find that, in time, you will get to recognise the wines you drink regularly – and any variations in them.

You will then soon be able to pick out wines from specific countries. Yes, Spanish wine really does have a distinctive smell and taste which separates it from French or Italian wine.

Think about how the wines from the New World are so distinctive. You probably wouldn't confuse them with European wine, would you? After this it's only a short step to starting to recognise grape varieties and their regional variations.

Colour

The first thing you see about a wine when you pour it out is its colour and, surprisingly, this can tell you quite a lot about the wine. Take white wine, for example. Most European wines are fairly pale in colour. Contrast this to the rich buttercup yellow of some of the white wines from Australia. So colour can give some indication of origin.

A darkish colouring in white wine can also mean old age or, even worse, oxidised wine. Oxidation occurs when a wine is badly stored and the cork has dried out. This allows the wine to come into contact with the air. To sort out which of these is causing the dark colour, you will have to resort to your sense of smell. Oxidised wine has a kind of sherry-like smell.

Sweet wines also tend to have a deep colour, but they will smell good and the sweetness will become immediately apparent when you come to taste it.

The colour of red wine can tell you rather more about its age. A young wine will have a purplish caste. As the wine matures the colour will change to plum, ruby and then reddish-brick. As it ages even further, the colour fades towards a brown brick colour.

This fading shows first as a brown or orange cast on the rim round the surface of the wine. The first hints of brown are often an indication that a fine wine is reaching its prime.

Smell

Trained wine tasters actually *smell* out almost everything about a wine and only use their sense of taste to confirm what their noses are telling them! On a less esoteric level your nose will immediately tell you if the wine is corked or has gone off in any way. Quite simply, it will smell horrible. So if you want to impress your friends in the local wine bar, don't bother to taste the wine, simply smell it before accepting or rejecting it.

Smells are difficult to describe, but the sherry-like smell of oxidised wine and the mouldy-mushroomy smell of corked wine are quite distinctive. Some people think that corked simply means broken cork in the wine, but in fact it describes a quite specific condition caused by a diseased cork.

On the more positive side, your sense of smell can certainly help you to identify the different grape varieties, as the most widely used ones have quite distinctive aromas. So, make a mental note when you next buy a French Sauvignon Blanc, such as Sancerre or Sauvignon de Touraine, and compare it with a Sauvignon from New Zealand. They won't smell exactly the same, but the underlying components will be similar.

Sauvigon Blanc is often described as having a herbaceous, minty or gooseberry-like aroma. Other common descriptions include blackcurrants for Cabernet Sauvignon, buttery or honeyed for Chardonnay, and grapey for Muscat wines. However, these are merely used as a shorthand for the memory, and if you think the wines smell of something else, use that as your personal benchmark for your next taste of the same variety.

Wines which have been aged in new oak barrels often take on a very distinctive vanilla-like smell. Think of Rioja or some of the Australian reds. And, as a general rule, young wines tend to taste more fruity than older wines.

Some wines don't give off very much smell at all. If they are fine red wines they may be going through a 'closed' period. This often happens after the first fruity aromas have worn off and before secondary components have had a chance to develop. Some cheaper wines also give off little aroma. This may not be a bad sign, but you will need to give even more attention to the taste.

Even if you don't want to become a wine buff, it does add a great deal of enjoyment if you take the trouble to smell the wine from time to time as you are drinking it.

Taste

The taste of the wine really confirms what your nose has already told you. The taste also tells you how dry or sweet the wine is, how sharp or acid it is, and how much tannin is present.

Young wines tend to be more acidic than older wines, but acidity is important in a wine. Of course, some wines have too much acidity; they are sharp and astringent and there are no fruity flavours to compensate. But a wine which has lost its acidity becomes very flat-tasting and this applies to medium and sweet wines as much as to dry wines.

Acidity is even more important in providing balance for a sweet wine, for without it the wine is cloying and unpleasant.

Tannin has a harsh taste and produces the feeling of a furry coating on the teeth. It is an essential element in a young wine which is expected to last, but you will have to decide for yourself how much tannin you are prepared to tolerate in cheaper wines which are ready to drink now. If there is little or no tannin in a wine, drink it at once.

For complete enjoyment of a wine, take time to think about the flavour that is left in the mouth after you have swallowed the wine. This is known as the 'finish' and in a really good wine it can linger for quite a while. Poor wines leave little or no taste. They may even leave a nasty taste!

Finally, consider the overall effect of the different aroma and taste sensations. Are they all in harmony or is one component more dominant than the others? A good wine should be in balance; it should offer a rounded and pleasing effect.

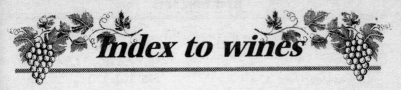

Index to wines